Serving the Oneness of Humanity

The Life of LOUIS GREGORY

By
Kiser Barnes and Linda Ahdieh Grant

BAHÁ'Í PUBLISHING
EVANSTON, ILLINOIS

Bahá'í Publishing
1233 Central St., Evanston, IL 60202

Printed in the United States of America ∞
28 27 26 25 1 2 3 4

Library of Congress Cataloging-in-Publication Data

Names: Barnes, Kiser D., author. | Grant, Linda Ahdieh, author.
Title: Serving the oneness of humanity : the life of Louis Gregory / by Kiser Barnes and Linda Ahdieh Grant.
Description: Evanston, IL : Bahá'í Publishing, 2025. | Includes bibliographical references.
Identifiers: LCCN 2025026568 (print) | LCCN 2025026569 (ebook) | ISBN 9781618512642 (paperback) | ISBN 9781618512659 (epub)
Subjects: LCSH: Gregory, Louis G. | Hands of the Cause of God—United States—Biography. | African American Bahais—Biography. | Bahais—United States—Biography. | Bahai Faith. | LCGFT: Biographies.
Classification: LCC BP395.G73 B376 2025 (print) | LCC BP395.G73 (ebook) | DDC 297.9/3092 [B]—dc23/eng/20250607
LC record available at https://lccn.loc.gov/2025026568
LC ebook record available at https://lccn.loc.gov/2025026569

Cover design by Carlos Esparza
Book design by Patrick Falso

Serving the Oneness of Humanity

This book is dedicated to Gayle Morrison with deep appreciations for her masterful studies of Mr. Louis Gregory's services and life.

CONTENTS

ACKNOWLEDGMENTS

In our considerations of some major features of the life and legacy of Louis George Gregory, a man of immense spiritual stature, a heroic trailblazer for racial unity and justice, our study of his unassailable commitment to the principle of the oneness of humanity and of his unique service to the ancient and universal ideal, Gayle Morrison's "pioneering,"[1] "excellent,"[2] and "illuminating"[3] biography was of inestimable value. We are greatly indebted to Dr. Morrison and wish to express to her our deepest appreciation for her masterful book.

Special thanks also to Janet Ruhe-Schoen, author of *Champions of Oneness: Louis Gregory and His Shining Circle;* to Richard Thomas for his articles in *Lights of the Spirits: Historical Portraits of Black Bahá'ís in North America 1898–2000;* to Louis Venters, author of *No Jim Crow Church: The Origins of South Carolina's Bahá'í Community;* to Fleming Rose, author of *A Seed in Your Heart: The Life of Louise Mathew Gregory;* to Doris McKay, author of *Fire in Many Hearts;* to Elsie Austin, author of *Above All Barriers: The Story of Louis G. Gregory;* and to Annette Reynolds, author of *Trudy and the Bahá'ís Spiritual Path in South Carolina;* for their distinguished books and articles regarding Mr. Gregory.

We are especially grateful for the loving support provided by our spouses, Nancy Park Barnes and Gavin Grant. We want to thank Kiser's children and their spouses—Theresa Clark, Tracey and Melvin Jackson, Dylan Elizabeth and Sherveen Lotfi, Jamal Martha Park and Morgan Evans, and Kiser Haydar Ali. We also want to thank Linda's children—Bahiyyih Amelia Grant and Thomas Vahid Grant. All have been a precious source of inspiration and encouragement.

Finally, our deepest gratitude goes to Christopher Martin, Associate Editor, for his efficient, encouraging, and amicable editing, which greatly improved this effort, and to other members of the Bahá'í Publishing Trust for their contributions.

INTRODUCTION

"In this illumined age that which is confirmed is the oneness of the world of humanity. Every soul who serveth this oneness will undoubtedly be assisted and confirmed."
—'Abdu'l-Bahá, *Selections from the Writings of 'Abdu'l-Bahá,* no. 77.1.

This book considers Louis George Gregory's unique and historic contributions toward advancing racial unity in America and beyond. These contributions were grounded in his full embrace of the teachings of the Bahá'í religion "directed toward . . . [the] spiritual transformation of both the individual and of society"[1] and the oneness of humanity, "the pivot round which all the teachings of Bahá'u'lláh revolve."[2] Louis Gregory fully realized that this reality held the potential to "alter completely the patterns of racial discrimination reinforced by class, caste, and religion in America and throughout the world and ultimately to create a new world civilization in which the characteristics and contributions of all peoples would play a part."[3] Louis Gregory himself asserted that what "'the majestic Revelation of Bahá'u'lláh brings . . . is not black or white or yellow or brown or red, yet all of these. It is the power of divine outpouring and endless perfection for mankind.'"[4]

He manifested commitment to this new Revelation in every facet of his adult life, including his marriage; his law practice; his heroic services spreading teachings of the Bahá'í Faith; his election as the first Black American member of the National Spiritual Assembly, the highest Bahá'í administrative institution in America; and his role as a key participant in Race Amity Conventions in cities throughout the country following a series of violent racial riots across the United States.

The Louis G. Gregory Public Museum at Charleston, South Carolina; the Louis G. Gregory Training Institute, a national educational center in Hemmingway, South Carolina; and the Louis G. Gregory Children's School in Eliot, Maine, are also inspiring and enduring testaments to Louis Gregory's lifelong belief that the transformation of society could be built on spiritual principles.

Of Louis Gregory's unique services, Glenford Mitchell has observed that "'Being one of the earliest Bahá'ís in America, Louis Gregory, the son of slaves, proved to be not only a luminous example in this sense but also, and more important, an instrument of change. His forty years of unremitting labor in promoting race amity was unprecedented in its scope, generated as it was by a universalism incomprehensible even to the most distinguished of the civil rights activists who were his contemporaries.'"[5]

The African-American lawyer, community activist, writer, newspaper editor, and lecturer was called by 'Abdu'l-Bahá—the leader of the Bahá'í Faith in the early 1900s—to "'become . . . the means whereby the white and colored people shall close their eyes to racial differences and behold the reality of humanity, and that is the universal unity which is . . . the basic harmony of the world . . .'"[6]

Louis Gregory clung to the Master's guidance.[7] He said of 'Abdu'l-Bahá, "'He is able to make all places fruitful'" and "'His is a wonderful culture of hearts and minds.'"[8] Janet Ruhe-Schoen wrote, "[Louis Gregory had] found the fulfillment of his heart's deepest desire, the longing that had entered him when he was a child in the midst of a violent tragedy." He wanted to help remove racial disunity, and he wanted humanity to be one, united in love.[9]

When he studied at Fisk University in Nashville, Tennessee and Howard University's law school in Washington, DC, Louis "placed his undiminished concern for the welfare of his people within a universal context: the establishment of a new world order founded, like the great civilizations of the past, on faith in a Supreme Being and on an ennobling vision of human destiny."[10]

He shared Bahá'í teachings with Blacks and whites in large cities and small towns throughout the country, particularly in the South, where "his advocacy of racial unity could easily have cost him his life."[11] According to Glenford Mitchell, "'The life of Louis Gregory produced the litmus test of the workability of the Bahá'í teachings in effecting race unity. The successful result of this unprecedented effort would be an example to all peoples for all time.'"[12] Louis Gregory had "lived his life in the forefront of a struggle that is still being waged" and "the immediacy of his example has the power to inform and to inspire."[13] He is described as "one of the spiritual giants of his era" and "an historic figure."[14] He was "'a unique instrument in the binding together'" of people of different races.[15]

Louis Gregory was among the first generation of African Americans born free in the United States after slavery ended. However, he suffered, throughout his long life, the lurking humiliations and pains of living in a society plagued by racism. After the Civil War, Blacks had hoped they would finally be free not only from slavery but also from racial prejudice. However, this initial hope was replaced by the gradual realization that new forms of dominance, based on notions of white supremacy, had become the new reality in American society. Still hopeful that the sufferings of Black people in America would eventually be removed, Blacks had continued singing from the Negro Spirituals: "I'm so glad trouble don't last always."[16] They continued, along with like-minded people of other races, to struggle against racial inequality.

Louis Gregory's parents and grandparents knew they needed to safeguard his well-being as much as possible. They had no public education and lived in poverty, and they knew protecting their child would be a challenge. They knew, for instance, that many Southern white people would subject him to mistreatments. Realizing that physical violence against him could occur along his dangerous journey from childhood to adulthood, his kinfolk tried to instill in his little heart the spiritual qualities of love, courage, resilience, and faith, so that racism would not break his spirit and cause him to lose sight of his inherent nobility. Louis appreciated that these values were needed for him to become "'a servant of humanity'" who would help spread the principle of "'the oneness of the entire human race.'"[17]

Louis Gregory was among the first of his race in the United States with the independent thinking and courage to embrace the Bahá'í teachings as a spiritual means for confronting racial prejudice with love and patience. He chose in 1909 to join this new multiracial religion with a strong determination to adhere to its teachings. However, he initially had reservations about proceeding with his membership. Despite the lofty teachings of the Faith, certain influential members of his Bahá'í community of Washington, DC rejected the ideal of racial equality.

Notwithstanding some initial misgivings, Louis Gregory refused to keep his Bahá'í affiliation private. He saw no personal, social, or professional advantages for doing so. He worked tirelessly alongside Black and white Bahá'ís to teach the principle of the oneness of humanity to receptive souls. As he studied more of the writings of the Faith, he discovered that "Bahá'u'lláh taught, that Religion is the chief foundation of Love and Unity and the cause of Oneness."[18]

Therefore, Louis Gregory felt he must help people from all strata of society, including Bahá'ís who had recognized Bahá'u'lláh as the latest Manifestation of God. Referring to the Bahá'í community, Shoghi Effendi wrote, "I cannot believe that those whose hearts have been touched by the regenerating influence of God's creative Faith in His day will find it difficult to cleanse their souls from every lingering trace of racial animosity."[19]

Louis Gregory took the principle of oneness as the bedrock of his personal identity and a mandate for action. He saw the urgency and the necessity of his serving the oneness of humanity, and he felt strongly that establishing this pivotal Bahá'í principle could be achieved together by Blacks and whites manifesting, as Shoghi Effendi described, "genuine love, extreme patience, true humility, consummate tact, sound initiative, mature wisdom, and deliberate, persistent, and prayerful effort"[20] along with other "exalted and dynamic virtues."[21] Louis believed that "'co-operation, mutuality, [and] service'" would "'move the world" toward unity.'"[22]

Louis Gregory was greatly inspired by 'Abdu'l-Bahá's and Shoghi Effendi's calls to action, and he closely followed their guidance and directions for achieving racial equality. He boldly spread the Bahá'í Faith's unifying message throughout the United States, particularly in the South. He shared with thousands of people across America, in Canada, Egypt, Palestine (Israel), Germany, London, Paris, and Haiti the need for racial harmony. Among the prominent African Americans whom Louis Gregory associated with during his teaching efforts were, for example, W. E. B. Du Bois, Booker T. Washington, George Washington Carver, Ida B. Wells, Robert Abbott, Alain Locke, and several high-ranking leaders of the National Association for the Advancement of Colored People.

The Bahá'í Faith is an independent world religion. It was established in Persia (now Iran) in 1844 by Bahá'u'lláh (1817–1892). He proclaimed that "The religion of God [is] . . . the surest of all means for the dawning of the light of unity amongst men."[23] Bahá'u'lláh spent forty years in prison and exile for His teachings. He appointed his eldest son, 'Abdu'l-Bahá, to succeed Him, and 'Abdu'l-Bahá was the head of the Faith from 1892 to 1921. 'Abdu'l-Bahá wrote, ". . . the Divine religions. . . . lead their true followers to . . . unflagging efforts in the service of mankind. . . . It is religion . . . which produces all human virtues, and it is these virtues which are the bright candles of civilization."[24]

'Abdu'l-Bahá emphasized the "'unity of races, making of all that dwell on earth peoples and kindreds of one race.'"[25] Before He passed away in 1921, 'Abdu'l-Bahá appointed His grandson Shoghi Effendi as Guardian and head of the Faith, and Shoghi Effendi served in this capacity until his passing in 1957. Writing of the ill-will that existed between Blacks and whites in the United States, Shoghi Effendi informed the American Bahá'í community's Interracial Teaching Committee in 1957 that "both sides have prejudices to overcome; one, the prejudice which is built up in the minds of a people who have conquered and imposed their will, and the other the reactionary prejudice of those who have been conquered and sorely put upon."[26] He affirmed that the purpose of life to a Bahá'í "'was to promote the oneness of mankind,'"[27] and that "Freedom from racial prejudice, in any of its forms, should, . . . be adopted as the watchword of the entire body of the American believers."[28]

Louis Gregory once wrote, "The new teachings of the new day are adequate for unity in all race relations. This work is one of the most needed and the most inviting for human service. . . . People born in an atmosphere of prejudice are not hopeless. Such conditions yield to spiritual training."[29] He also wrote, "The work of overcoming [racial prejudice] is full of hope, and adds immeasurably to the joy of life."[30] He believed that

> Light is everywhere breaking for the oppressed peoples of the earth. . . . Deep shadows prove the intensity of the light. The interests of no groups or classes will be overlooked or forgotten. The wish of the underprivileged to be treated as fairly as are other Americans in every avenue of human advancement is both proper and reasonable. Untenable is the attitude of those who would withhold it because of complexion or other superficial reasons. The friends of the oppressed show rapid increase in numbers and powers. Assuming that the victims of injustice will continue their struggle, no human might can long debar them from the long sought goal. Earth and air, fire and water, the stars in their courses, the high tide of destiny, and the Will of divine Providence are all arrayed against the forces of oppression.[31]

Louis Gregory was likely inspired by 'Abdu'l-Bahá's message that ". . . mere knowledge is not sufficient for complete human attainment. The teachings of the Holy Books need a heavenly power and divine potency to carry them out. A house is not built by mere acquaintance with the plans. . . . volition is necessary to construct it; a carpenter must be employed in its erection. It is not enough to say, 'The plan and purpose of this house are very good; I will live in it.' . . . the house must be actually built before we can live in it."[32]

As discussed more fully below, Shoghi Effendi appointed Louis Gregory posthumously (after his passing in 1951) "Hand of the Cause of God,"[33] the highest appointive position in the Bahá'í Faith. Shoghi Effendi wrote to him, "'You have attained spiritual heights that few indeed can claim to have scaled. You have displayed a spirit that few, if any, can equal.'"[34]

Here are some ideals, from the Bahá'í writings that likely inspired Louis Gregory's services:

> In the estimation of God, there is no distinction of color; all are one in the color and beauty of servitude to Him. Color is not important; the heart is all-important . . .[35]

> He whose morals and virtues are praiseworthy is preferred. . . .[36]

> All colors are acceptable unto Him, be they white, black, or yellow. Inasmuch as all were created in the image of God, we must bring ourselves to realize that all embody divine possibilities.[37]

> The diversity in the human family should be the cause of love and harmony, as it is in music where many different notes blend together in the making of a perfect chord.[38]

The following words by his former law partner, James A. Cobb, offer a glimpse into his impressions of Louis Gregory: "'I knew him as a student, teacher, practicing lawyer, lecturer and friend, and in each capacity he was strong and outstanding. . . . [H]e was a fine student, a lovely character and a person with a great mind which he devoted to the betterment of mankind. . . . [T]hose with whom he came in contact were and are better for their association with him. In fact, he was one of those who enriched the life of America.'"[39]

1

STARTING FROM HOME: A GOOD BEGINNING

In 1910, Louis Gregory, a son of former slaves and a prominent lawyer in Washington, DC, shared several Bahá'í teachings that address racial prejudice with hundreds of people in eight segregated southern cities and towns. The teaching tour included visits to Richmond, Virginia; Durham, North Carolina; Charleston, South Carolina; and Macon, Georgia.[1]

Louis was determined to fulfill 'Abdu'l-Bahá's hope that he would become "'the means whereby the white and colored people shall close their eyes to racial differences'" and be "'the cause of the guidance of both races.'"[2] When Shoghi Effendi succeeded 'Abdu'l-Bahá in 1921 as head of the Bahá'í Faith, Louis also followed his guidance and instructions, believing that the Faith's teachings nourished peoples' hopes and dreams that racial equality could be achieved.

Louis' extensive teaching tour was a critical, unqualified success, a major achievement. He spoke directly to about nine hundred people in homes, social events, schools, and churches. Even though Black people were regarded with contempt and considered inferior to white people, audiences were nevertheless receptive to the Bahá'í teaching that love and unity were the central purposes of all religions. In many cities, Louis secured positive newspaper coverage about his journey.[3]

Lecturing on the tour was hard work, but Louis loved it, and he never tired of it. He informed Pauline and Joseph Hannen, a white Bahá'í couple in Washington, DC, who had collaborated with him over the groundbreaking foray: "'Am just having the time of my life!'" He would further say, "'Have many engagements to speak, in churches and at gatherings, on Bahaism [the Bahá'í Faith].'"[4]

The tour demonstrated that Louis had broadened his spiritual identity. He had realized that spreading knowledge about the Faith was an important, sacred duty for every Bahá'í. During his travels, Louis also shared the central Bahá'í teaching that all the Prophets had been sent to humanity by God for the unification of all people and races.

Numerous speaking engagements in Black churches likely helped inspire his approval, years later, of W. E. B. DuBois' view of the role of religion in strengthening Blacks in the United States. In a book review of one of DuBois' essays,[5] Louis wrote, "The Negro is inseparable from his religion. It colors all his stations. . . . all his activities. . . . How would the black man . . . . support existence or even attain it, without a hold upon God? His religion is the major part of his history . . . . [and] the major note of his song."[6]

Having experienced prejudice from childhood, "'he wanted to do something, get ahold of something'" to satisfy his yearning to help remove hatred between Blacks and whites.[7] As stated above, the Bahá'í Faith became "the major part of his history" and his "hold upon God" through recognition of Bahá'u'lláh as the Prophet-Founder of the Bahá'í Faith. His teachings gave Louis a spiritual foundation for advancing freedom from all forms of prejudice.

Although Louis was deeply committed to advocating for the rights of Blacks in the United States, he never lost his focus on the importance of unity between the races. Gayle Morrison writes, "Wherever he went, with whomever he was, however deeply he was concerned with the universal view, he never allowed anyone to forget his particular commitment to the cause of oneness."[8] On one occasion, he addressed Bahá'í teachings to over a hundred ministers. Their bishop had ordered them to open their pulpits to him.[9] However, in Charleston a prominent Black minister criticized him and his religion. He based his "scathing denunciation" on what Louis had said about interracial unity during his 1910 visit.[10]

In his efforts to share his belief in the oneness of humanity, Louis participated in the prestigious African American Literary and Historical Society intellectual forums in Washington, DC. His close consultation with others helped to promote the Bahá'í-sponsored "Race Amity Conventions." He also associated with the southern-based Commission on Interracial Cooperation and the National Association for the Advancement of Colored People (NAACP), formed in 1909. He was present when 'Abdu'l-Bahá addressed the fourth annual conference of the Association.[11] He corresponded, for example, with W. E. B. DuBois, Booker T. Washington, George Washington Carver, and Alain Locke. Additionally, he made several uplifting presentations throughout America, Canada, Germany, London, and Paris,[12] as well as in Palestine (Israel),[13] and published several brilliant works, among them the essay "Racial Amity in America: An Historical Review."[14]

As a result of his trailblazing service, Louis was elected and appointed to several Bahá'í administrative positions. He was, for example, the first Black person elected to the National Spiritual Assembly of the Bahá'ís of the United States and Canada.[15] He also served on the National Spiritual Assembly's Race Unity Committee from 1939 until 1947, when the committee was discontinued.[16] These were remarkable, progressive achievements at a time when Black persons seldom held leadership positions in white-majority organizations.

Louis Gregory was born June 6, 1874 in Charleston, South Carolina, to Mary Elizabeth and Ebenezer George, nine years after the Civil War effectively ended. His parents and grandparents were among four million Black people freed from slavery, which had existed since 1619 in an endemically prejudiced American society.[17]

Photo of Louis as a young man, date unknown.
(US Bahá'í National Archives)

He was born during the short period of Reconstruction aimed at reforming Southern whites' practices toward Black people. However, new barriers to racial equality were erected. Prior to 1874, the family had moved to Charleston from the Darlington District, some 120 miles north of Charleston in the Pee Dee section.[18] They had relocated with Louis' brother, Theodore, and their grandmother, Mary Bacot. It was a time of deep poverty and, for many Black families, even hunger.

His parents and grandparents knew they must make Louis and Theodore strong inside with religious qualities, so that the humiliating conditions of racial subjugation wouldn't destroy their inborn nobility. Within their tiny home, with no electricity or running water, they "schooled" Louis in "qualities necessary to overcome a black man's humiliating lot" in a racist society: courage, self-respect, dignity, assurance, resourcefulness, a sense of humor, the love of laughter, and the love of learning.[19]

One quality connected everyone in Louis' family. It was an overarching, suffusing, uplifting force. It was the virtue of love. Louis demonstrated its force so fully that following his extraordinary services to human oneness as a Bahá'í, Shoghi Effendi wrote that he showed a "'shining love'" for all people.[20] He learned that love, and every other virtue, must be manifested in action. One can easily imagine his parents and grandparents holding him very tenderly; their faces lit with a smiling gladness; their wondering eyes looking into his; their soft laughter; their sweet kisses on his little cheeks; their singing; their gentle swaying as they held Louis—perhaps, sometimes, with chuckling lifts into the air; and their inspired and imploring words.

Apparently, to help him appreciate why compliance with his elders' higher wisdom and direction was critical, his grandmother told him why white supremacists had murdered her husband. A former Union soldier, he was a successful blacksmith with his own mule and horse, but his achievements had infuriated some Ku Klux Klan members. One night they rode up on their horses and called him out of his home. When he bravely came out, they shot him, then rode away.[21]

No wonder Morrison writes that Louis "gained as a child . . . a keen sense of the injustices his people continued to face."[22] Louis said his grandmother told him the tragic story without harsh or hateful words against her husband's murderers. Her sense of nobility had assisted her in overcoming her shock, her pain, and her grief.[23] Her acceptance of and peace with her husband's death was "[h]er final answer" to the killers.[24] Maybe she was the kind of grandmother many children long to have, one who could find hope even in the face of tragedy.

As mentioned in the previous chapter, Louis' kin knew that schooling him in values was the foundation for building a strong moral character. They had faith that teaching their son how to live a good life would fortify him so that a hostile, segregated society would not be able to break his innate sense of nobility, and they believed that drawing on the strength of biblical teachings would teach Louis the values that would assist him to triumph over the divisive forces surrounding him.

Mary Bacot raised a grandson who, like her, would not be frightened into wrong thinking and wrong acting. She taught him to love rather than to hate, to be courageous, to forgive, and to persevere so that he would never give up on achieving his hopes and dreams. Most importantly, she taught him spiritual nobility, and perhaps her lofty instructions affirmed the biblical phrase "For out of the abundance of the heart the mouth speaketh."[25]

He asserted that religious values inspired and directed his whole life.

Louis never got a "big head," as he called it. Doris McKay writes in her book *Fires in Many Hearts* that once when he and other adults were discussing the need to manifest spiritual attributes, he astonished everyone. A participant recalled that Louis said, "‘"Let me tell you that in my youth, my greatest sin was pride."’"[26] Everyone was amused by his statement because, as this individual recounted, "‘Louis was a most humble and self-effacing man. So humble was he that we all laughed heartily at the "monster of self" that we imagined him to have slain. Louis laughed too, and mocked the situation by getting down on his knees and begging for help.'"[27] The participant recalled that Louis continued in a more serious vein, "'"We have to look at ourselves first and bring ourselves to account so that we will know when we are 'standin' in need of prayer."'"[28]

From the values instilled in him by his family, Louis learned that love was a magnificent source of unlimited strength. He put it this way: "[W]hoever learns to love and praise people for whatever tokens [qualities] of the Creator they show has discovered an impregnable fortress of strength."[29] He always found, within himself, the strength to love.

His family also strove to cultivate in him a deeply ingrained habit of self-effacement. He recalled that his father, was "'regular in habits, thrifty in living and pious in life.'" Like his grandmother, his father also placed great emphasis on learning biblical teachings and spending time together as a family, and he often drove his family out together "'after the Sunday worship, which followed the week of toil.'"[30]

Louis's grandmother's formidable strength of character no doubt came from the hardships she had endured during her life. As a young girl, she had been stolen from her African village and forced to endure the voyage via a slave ship to North America. Frightened and alone, she had been taken to the Charleston area, where she was sold to George Washington Dargan. A white descendant of Irish immigrants, he was a lawyer, a judge, and a state Senator who held at least 119 Blacks as slaves on his plantation. With absolute dominion over all his slaves, he forced Louis' grandmother to be his defenseless, compelled, "slave-wife," and Louis' mother was their daughter.[31]

As slaves, mother and daughter were Dargan's property and subject to his every command. Louis was always proud that his grandmother was, as he described her, "wholly of African blood."[32] Mr. Dargan died in 1859. Even though he was separated from his white relatives by barriers of caste, Louis never resented his mixed heritage. Gayle Morrison writes, "His upbringing also prepared him to build bridges of racial understanding. In his experience, whites were not simply the oppressors; they were also his forbears, playmates, teachers, and friends. He gained as a child both a keen sense of the injustices his people continued to face and an understanding that whites were, in a broader sense, his people, too."[33] She continues, "With characteristic dignity, Louis Gregory rejected bitterness over the manifold wrongs of the past."[34] Louis himself wrote, after becoming a member of the Bahá'í Faith, "'I did not choose them [the Dargan family] as my forebears, but in justice must acknowledge my obligations to them.'"[35] He always chose love over hate in every situation.

His grandmother's magnanimous spirit helped shape his positive attitude toward his white relatives. The word *magnanimous* comes from Latin, and it means *a great soul.* It describes someone who is big-hearted, generous, noble, brave, loving, and forgiving. Louis' grandmother had a magnanimous spirit, and so did Louis.

Louis also possessed a good sense of humor. His grandmother used her great sense of humor in her storytelling and her nursing services, and Louis said she was "'the only person that I have ever known who could make me laugh beyond all control.'"[36] Morrison writes that "The amusement his grandmother found even in plantation life helped to make bearable both past and present indignities, the painful memories of slavehood and the harsh realities of emancipation."[37] Morrison further writes that humor "served to lighten many difficulties [for Louis] in the years ahead" and "became a valuable asset in his racial amity work."[38] It was a "source of strength and balance."[39] So confident was Louis in laughter's healing power that he wrote, after he began his career in 1909 promoting interracial unity: "'If the walls of caste are ever to be shattered, laughter . . . will be no small power in such a change.'"[40] His good humor helped him look to the future.

Louis became a great storyteller, with lots of tales and a marvelous, ringing laugh. Roy Williams, a young Black Bahá'í in Washington, DC whom Louis mentored, observed: "'He [Louis] was a very affable man and . . . he could tell simple, homespun stories . . . that would keep the other people present . . . roaring with laughter.'" His charm was in his "'humility, his utter disregard of arrogance and ostentation, his smiling happy face—no complaints, no criticism, no idea of the superiority of his position as an excellent lawyer, . . .'"[41] Louis and Roy had many happy, laughing times together advancing racial amity. They also faced some unpleasant times during their Southern teaching journeys.

In 1879, when Louis was five years old, his father died of tuberculosis. In 1881, when he was seven, his mother remarried, and her new husband was George Gregory. He was a literate freeborn native of Charleston. He, too, had a good sense of humor. He was a very good father to Louis and Theodore, who was four years older. Louis became Louis George Gregory. In 1890, Theodore died of pneumonia. The following year, Louis' mother died of spinal meningitis. Mr. Gregory remained a caring father for the rest of his life.

2

EDUCATION: A LEVER FOR SOCIAL CHANGE

When Louis started primary school, he had already made up his mind that he would study hard. He hoped, through education, to be able to acquire the tools that would allow him to confront the racial prejudice and injustices he saw around him every day. He resolved not to allow the segregation of the public school system to hold him back from achieving his goals. He had a vision of using education to help others,[1] and in his childhood, he was recognized as highly intelligent.[2]

Many white Southerners believed, however, that giving Black children access to public education would threaten the privileges and powers that were enjoyed by many whites. Racist officials and citizens were determined that Black students would only receive an inferior education, if any. Some officials believed that Blackness even constituted a learning disability. Louis Gregory later dismissed this thinking in this way: "As no one chooses his own color at birth," "color" is no "test" for "ability" or "character."[3]

In 1865, the federal Freedmen's Bureau was established. It created, supervised, and supported numerous primary schools, high schools, and colleges throughout the South. Its mission was to provide relief and help formerly enslaved people become self-sufficient.[4] Louis was one of the many beneficiaries of this agency, as he was among the first generation of African Americans to obtain public education in South Carolina in primary school. His high school, the Avery Normal Institute, was founded in Charleston in 1865 and was established by the American Missionary Association.[5] When he obtained his bachelor's degree from Fisk University in 1896, he returned home to teach at Avery and to be the editor of a weekly newspaper, the *Afro-Americana Citizen*.[6]

Throughout Louis' educational experiences, numerous racist campaigns against the education of Black children were mounted by white citizens from all strata of society. Especially in the South, schools and most other public places were segregated by laws that seemed designed to humiliate Blacks. Blacks couldn't walk on the same staircase with white people and had to step off the sidewalk to allow a white person to pass. They also couldn't use the same public conveniences as whites and could only eat in designated restaurants or in parts of a restaurant that were blocked off from white people. Additionally, Black people were forced to sit in segregated places on public buses and trains. The consequence was, as Janet Ruhe-Schoen points out, "Every African American child, born carefree, as his human birthright, had his or her moment of pain and shame when the truth struck and wounded him or her. 'You do not belong. You are not good. You are other.' The wounding and re-wounding went on for life."[7]

A sensitive child, Louis could sense that many of his white teachers in the schools he attended in Charleston wanted their Black students to succeed. Somehow, they had managed to overcome the ingrained racial prejudice of the culture in which they lived. According to Janet Ruhe-Schoen, Louis found that the professors and administrators at Avery and other schools along with the founders of the schools, "exemplified the American tradition of race amity—whites reaching out to people of color to help and assuage—that had always run counter to slave-holding and segregationist policies in the United States."[8] Louis wrote that at Fisk University, the white professors and administrators "'sacrificed income and position to devote their lives to the children of former slaves.'"[9]

Despite the often-strained relationship between the school staff and their Black students, Louis respected his teachers and admired their professionalism.[10] Louis' schoolteachers were almost always white. Even so, he recalled that the principal of the Simonton school, an ex-Confederate soldier, was "'a fine disciplinarian and highly polished gentleman who loved his task and did it well. Likewise efficient were the teachers who served with him and well trained for their task.'"[11] But "'the time came, none too early, when the colored people were engaged by the Board of Education to man their own schools.'"[12]

During this time, certain established patterns of racial segregation in American society were in the process of being dismantled, and these changes no doubt resulted in some of the uneasiness between Black students and their white teachers. Some of it may have come from memories, from both sides, of Black protests against subjugation. For example, all students and teachers in Charleston probably knew of Denmark Vesey's story. A free Black carpenter and community leader in Charleston, he was accused in 1822 of planning to free some slaves. During a secret trial, Vesey and other Black defendants were not permitted to confront their accusers, nor were they allowed to hear any testimony against them. The state's governor and attorney general believed the proceedings were unfair and illegal, especially since the accused faced possible executions, and they felt that the defendants should have been permitted to confront their accusers' charges.[13]

Vesey and five other slaves were found guilty, and they were executed by hanging on July 2, 1822. Thirty Blacks were executed later, and city authorities ordered Vesey's church razed. Fears of another slave revolt led to increased restrictions on both enslaved and free Blacks.[14]

Louis traced his resolve to obtain a good education back to one person: George Gregory, his stepfather. He strengthened Louis' "insatiable taste for education."[15] He never failed in his love for his stepson, and he was among the African Americans who understood that education was a lever for advancing racial progress and for changing the world.[16] Mr. Gregory's character and achievements gave Louis a sense of pride, and his love, nobility, and moderate habits greatly influenced Louis.[17]

Mr. George Gregory hated slavery and never owned slaves. Some Black freemen did, but Mr. Gregory always vigorously advocated for freedom for everyone. He was an influential Black community leader in Charleston. A literate carpenter with a strong sense of humor, he served in the 104th Regiment U.S. Colored Infantry during the Civil War, and he was able to build financial security for his family and enjoy the benefits that came from his military service.[18] Some of Louis' earliest playmates included children of white Northern troops stationed in Charleston. While playing with them, Gayle Morrison writes that Louis "gained perhaps his first experiences of interracial amity."[19]

Mr. Gregory's resolve to provide Louis with an education was fulfilled in several ways. With a practical sensibility for Louis' future financial welfare, he found an apprenticeship for Louis to learn to become a tailor.[20] Tradesmen were respected and admired in Black communities, and among the seven hundred employed free African Americans in Charleston before the Civil War, one hundred twenty-two were carpenters, eighty-seven were tailors, thirty were shoemakers, eighteen were bricklayers, twenty-three were butchers, ten were bootmakers, and eleven were painters.[21]

Louis was proud to be a tailor, and he never looked down on any class or profession. After his stepfather financed his first year of college at Fisk University, Louis worked his way through college by tailoring, mending, cleaning, and pressing clothes for fellow students.[22]

Knowing that Black men and women had struggled for their freedom from slavery, Mr. George Gregory probably knew of Robert Smalls' spectacular escape from slavery in 1862, and he may have told the story to Louis.

Smalls, a twenty-three-year-old enslaved Black harbor pilot, stood aboard a Confederate gunboat one night. When his three commanding white officers were ashore during the early morning, he plotted his escape. Wearing a captain's uniform, Smalls cranked up the vessel's engines and began to pilot the gunboat in the moonlit waters toward the promise of freedom. Guiding the ship past Confederate forts and issuing checkpoint signals, he steamed up the Cooper River. He stopped at a wharf to pick up his wife, child, and his Black crew's families. In the dawn's light, with a white sheet on the gunboat to serve as a surrender flag, Smalls reached his selected destination—the Union Navy blockade around Charleston harbor. Officers aboard a Union ship were about to give the order to fire on the gunboat when a crewman spotted the white flag. Union sailors then boarded the gunboat, and Smalls saluted them. He told them, "I am delivering this war material including these cannons and I think Uncle (President) Abraham Lincoln can put them to good use." Through his courage, perseverance, and level-headedness, Smalls had successfully gained freedom for himself and his family, and for his crew of seven slaves and their families as well.[23]

After this escape, Smalls joined the Union army and eventually earned the rank of captain. After the Civil War, he became a U.S. Congressman and a member of the South Carolina Senate. He died in 1915. His example of courage and intelligence inspired many. He showed that the indomitable spirit of the Black race, with its struggle for freedom and equality in the United States, could not be broken.[24]

Mr. George Gregory's legacy gave Louis a sense of pride and self-worth. Their close and loving association played a large part in Louis' learning "qualities necessary" to overcome "a black man's humiliating lot" in a racist society.[25] As stated earlier, these qualities included self-respect, a love of learning, assurance, dignity, resourcefulness, and a sense of humor. As he grew older, Louis would appreciate the value of these principles that his father had taught him.

Louis graduated from Fisk University in 1896, and he returned home to teach for a time at Avery Normal Institute, his Black high school. He took initiative to study law at Howard University's Law School. In 1902, he gave the commencement address, titled "The Growth of Peace Laws." The address emphasized the importance of the development of international peace laws and disarmament, and it may have foreshadowed his later appreciation for the Bahá'í teachings, which state that the accomplishment of interracial unity "'will be an assurance of the world's peace'" and that racial prejudice will eventually "'pass away and remain no longer.'"[26] In subsequent years, Louis would begin to understand that the principle of human oneness was not a "vague and pious hope,"[27] and his brilliant academic achievements would serve him well in the years to come as a Bahá'í "spokesman for racial unity."[28]

Soon after his graduation from law school, Louis began practicing law in Washington, DC. What a magnificent achievement for a son of former slaves! He, like other Black lawyers, was considered a "champion" of Black people's "rights," and a sort of "legal Moses" who would lead Black people "to the land of freedom and promise."[29] He did not know that he would soon champion a universal movement toward freedom from all forms of prejudice.

Glenford Mitchell, in the Foreword to Gayle Morrison's *To Move the World,* has noted that Mr. Gregory

> was instrumental in demonstrating the Faith's relevance to the civil rights movement and in winning the sympathy of the movement's [NAACP] leaders for the new religion he had embraced by unveiling to them its all-encompassing spirit . . . Bahá'ís lent substantial moral support to the organizations heading the struggle for black rights . . . It does not diminish the importance of the civil rights movement in America to say that Mr. Gregory's beliefs and actions encompassed its stated goals; for the movement reflects the spirit of change that is the avowed purpose of the Bahá'í Faith to bring about in human affairs . . . It was not so much that the path he chose was different in purpose from that embarked upon by the civil rights movement initiated at the beginning of the century by Mr. DuBois and others; it was simply that both he and they had different but indispensable components of the same goal to attain . . . For even after every civil right has been legally

Photo of Louis as a young man, date unknown. (US Bahá'í National Archives)

secured for the black or any other minority, there will yet remain the elusive goal of uniting that minority spiritually and socially with all other peoples on the planet. In this light, Mr. Gregory's example remains integral to any effort designed to remove racial barriers.[30]

3

TRUTH HAD A HEARING

On a cold, dark, wet, and stormy night in 1907, Louis attended his first Bahá'í meeting in Washington, DC. As he walked through the slashing rain to the meeting, he could only feel despair over the racial conflict in the United States. As a graduate of two outstanding Black universities, a resident in the national capital, and a trained lawyer who had close interactions with Black intellectuals and activists, he was keenly aware of both the hostile and constructive forces affecting Black people.[1]

He knew that lingering suspicions and misunderstandings, which underscored the need for social change, still existed between the races. He also was aware he had reached a point in his life in which he could become, if he wished, more involved in political, legal, and social movements for constructive change.[2]

Despite the prejudice he had experienced in Charleston, Louis loved the South and felt it had great potential to heal racial divisions. Once he observed that "'the feelings of illwill,'" some whites held against Black people were "'not universal'" throughout the region. He continued, "'I cannot recall a time when at least some whites of the South could not be found who were willing for the colored race to have every right and opportunity, on the basis of merit, which they themselves enjoyed. That minority has grown with the passing years and that it will become a majority ere long is as certain as the sunrise. . . .'"[3]

Louis knew much about racial prejudice, but he was still groping for ways in which he might help eliminate it. He thought he might design a strategy which would advance what Glenford Mitchell referred to as Louis' "'somewhat radical allegiance to the cause of Negro rights.'"[4]

Louis opened a law office in 1902 with James A. Cobb, who was also a graduate of Howard University's School of Law. In 1904, Louis argued the case of Barney McKay—a Black former cavalry soldier, newspaper editor, and Republican activist—that involved charges against a white innkeeper for assault and violation of the District of Columbia's civil rights laws. Another time, he and another Black attorney staged a sit-down protest against a segregated white-only lunchroom in Washington's City Hall and "put their bodies on the line."[5] These were brave actions for social change.

After his partnership with Mr. Cobb ended in 1906, Louis worked in the law division of the US Treasury Department and shared an office with two elderly white colleagues. One was Mr. Thomas Gibbs, who, according to Louis Gregory, was "'intensely Southern in his sympathies and outlook on life.'"[6] The other, whom Louis described as "'a fine representative of . . . his state with its traditions of justice and freedom,'" was from Massachusetts.[7] Conversing with Louis, they found he was engaging and always had something to say in his soft, mellow voice that had a slight Southern accent. As Louis put it, in those days he was "'quite disputatious.'"[8]

Louis wrote many years later that any question about the Civil War would bring his two office mates into verbal conflict. However, something strange happened when he began presenting them with ideas he had formulated for dealing with racial prejudice. He outlined strategies, which called for full civil and political rights for African Americans and for ending racial prejudice and injustice, developed by Black and white activists. He wrote later, "'[T]hese men (his two co-workers) were very indulgent to me because of my youth and inexperience.'" He further recalled, "'They listened with patience to ideas of mine which were wild-eyed and radical'" and "'read articles of mine and others, offered [to] them.'" Despite their patience with Louis, his two colleagues still rejected his proposed program of "'fiery agitation in behalf of a people'" and were of the opinion that such ideas "'would avail nothing in the removal of such wrongs, but would rather move friends and foes to combine against me.'"[9]

Louis' "'attitude'" to his office mates' personal views was "'unyielding.'" He never thought of himself as an expert for removing racial prejudice, nor was he prejudiced against white people. His family had taught him better than that. He said that his colleagues "'spoke soothingly when my feelings, as not infrequently happened, were ruffled.'" They showed him, he said, "'deep interest and kindness.'"[10] He also indicated that he was struck by their "'patience,'" "'friendship,'" and "'affection.'" Always a humble learner, he listened and learned. Their frank and honest personal views made, as he stated, "'an indelible impression upon my life.'"[11]

He found it amazing that Gibbs invited him to his home for dinner. It meant Gibbs and his wife regarded him as their equal. Gayle Morrison wrote that it was an "unprecedented" event in Louis' entire life experience.[12] The rarity of such an occurrence—a white man inviting a Black man for dinner—illustrates how deeply entrenched racial prejudice had become in American culture.

Louis recalled that Gibbs insisted that he attend a Bahá'í meeting. Gibbs was not a Bahá'í, and although he had attended a few Bahá'í meetings, he was not seriously interested in the religion. The little he knew of it, however, he liked, and he thought its teachings might appeal to Louis. For his part, Louis thought he would attend a meeting only as a "'favor'" to Gibbs.[13] Even though Louis doubted anything would come from his attending the meeting, he was still courteous to his colleague. As he walked through the storm to the meeting that night, perhaps the storm was mirroring the racial disunity he had witnessed throughout his life and the despair he was feeling in his heart.

Louis was an agnostic, and while he was spiritual, he was not religious. He had lost interest in religion because, in his words, he "'had been seeking, but not finding truth, [and he] had given up.'"[14] Instead, he had placed his faith in an essentially secular approach for combating racial oppression.

Photo of Louis, date unknown.
(US Bahá'í National Archives)

He was welcomed by Pauline Hannen, a white woman who was there. He later recounted that she identified him as Mr. Gibbs' friend and gave him "'an unusually cordial welcome.'" She then suggested he "'would hear something very wonderful, though difficult.'" Louis recounted, "'She urged me to get a full understanding of the message . . . that through it a work would be possible that would bless humanity.'"[15]

The next to arrive was Lua Getsinger. Louis Venters writes, "Although she held no particular rank in the religion . . . she was among the most knowledgeable Bahá'ís in the United States" of its teachings and among those "most active in its propagation."[16] Lua gave a "'brief but vivid'" introduction to the Bahá'í Faith, and she spoke about the persecutions against it in Persia.[17]

Louis was intrigued by what he had heard from Lua. At the end of the meeting, Pauline gave him an English translation of Bahá'u'lláh's ethical writings titled The Hidden Words.[18] It had transformed Pauline.[19] It consists of short verses on the moral and spiritual essence of religion, for "the reorientation of the minds of men, the edification of their souls and the rectification of their conduct. . . ."[20] Within those scriptures, Bahá'u'lláh proclaimed that all people were "created . . . from the same dust . . . [t]hat no one should exalt himself over the other."[21]

Pauline also gave him an introductory book called *The Dawn of Knowledge and the Most Great Peace* by Paul K. Dealy. This book considered the Bahá'í Faith in relation to the fulfillment of biblical prophecies.[22]

At her invitation, Louis attended a second Bahá'í meeting, then another, and many more. In those Sunday evening meetings in Pauline's home, he felt so welcomed that he brought some of his Black friends with him. He later recalled, "'The light they [the Hannens] unfolded was so wonderful that for about a year we sat in dumb amazement, listening to their patient, loving talks, not knowing whether to advance or retreat, yet held by supernal power.'"[23]

Louis had come upon the Bahá'í Faith inadvertently and had attended his first meeting reluctantly. Gradually, he realized that the Faith was the truth he had previously given up finding. In the Hannens' home, he must have felt in his healing heart something of the gladness he had experienced in Thomas Gibbs' home. Against all odds, what might be thought of as little ideas, little kindnesses, little coincidences, were being sown deeply in Louis' heart.

After eighteen months of serious study with Pauline and Joseph Hannen,[24] he became "a confirmed believer" in June 1909.[25] He said, "'my mental veils were cleared away and the light of assurance mercifully appeared within.'"[26] Those veils had made him, so to speak, wander far from home.

Louis wrote, "'It [The Bahá'í Revelation] has given me an entirely new conception of Christianity and of all religion, and with it my whole nature seems changed for the better.'"[27] The Words of God he had considered in the Hannens' study class, and his own personal reflections, had rung true to him. Gayle Morrison has stressed that Louis "saw it [the Bahá'í Faith] . . . as a remedy for the plight of black Americans."[28]

Louis always remembered that incredible beginning of his spiritual journey—so much so that Gayle Morrison observed, "It is doubtful whether anyone, black or white, could have changed the focus of Louis Gregory's 'radical' ideas, made an impression on his 'unyielding attitude,' or renewed his belief in religion, if his 'unreconstructed' Southern friend, Thomas H. Gibbs, had not become, as Mr. Gregory described him, 'the means of guiding me to the spiritual forces which for many years have directed my life.'"[29] Louis also expressed his gratitude to Pauline and Joseph Hannen in these words: "'I shall always remember with deepest gratitude. . . . the zeal, enthusiasm, love, attraction & wisdom of my spiritual parents when they guided me gently to the Path of El Abha [Baha'u'llah].'"[30] In July 1909, he again thanked Pauline and Joseph Hannen for "'all your kindness and patience, which finally culminated in my acceptance of the great truths of the Bahá'í Revelation. . . . It is a sane and practical religion, which meets all the varying needs of life, and I hope I shall ever regard it as a priceless possession.'"[31]

His grandmother had always taught him to respect and admire good character and good conduct. He had followed her guidance, and in doing so, he had found his way back home. It was a spiritual home, with room enough for people of all colors and creeds.

As previously described, Louis wrote that his colleagues at work had "'made an indelible impression upon my life.'" Thinking and acting anew, he observed, "'they were both to me warm personal friends such as I hope never to forget in time or eternity.'"[32] He had learned that investigating the reality of religion could be life changing. He had followed Bahá'u'lláh's guidance from The Hidden Words to "see with thine own eyes and not through the eyes of others," and to "know of thine own knowledge and not through the knowledge of thy neighbor."[33]

Morrison has observed that 'Abdu'l-Bahá "found in Louis Gregory a willing pupil—thoughtful, well-educated, articulate, humble, bridging in his own upbringing the formidable chasm of legal and de facto segregation that separated black and white Americans in his day. . . . Although he was neither the first of his race to become a Bahá'í in America nor the most outstanding black intellectual, he won dual distinction as a leader and as a spokesman for racial unity."[34]

Louis had become spiritually strong as his family had hoped. He could walk through the inevitable storms he would encounter with the strength of love, continuing his journey toward becoming a luminous star—a champion for human oneness.

4

A SPIRITUAL FOUNDATION FOR ADVANCING HUMAN ONENESS

At the age of thirty-five, Louis Gregory fully embraced the principle of the oneness and wholeness of humankind, even though at that time, white supremacist ideas and a conviction of Black inferiority still permeated American society, including its white religious culture. He recognized, however, that all whites in the South didn't dislike Black people. In fact, some had a deep and abiding affection for Blacks.[1] He also knew there was so much woven into the fabric of American society, even in its religious communities, that branded Blacks insignificant.

Mr. George Gregory, Louis' stepfather, did not follow Louis into the Bahá'í Faith. At the age of eighty-seven, Mr. George Gregory died in 1929. On one occasion, he wrote Louis, "'I am glad to hear from you all your travels. You seem to be going all over the Country. . . . I hope you may live long to do good for the Master (one of 'Abdu'l-Bahá's titles). . . . God bless you and [your] wife. I am praying for you both.'"[2]

Indeed, as early as 1910, Louis undertook a teaching tour of the Southern states. He often returned to the South, and he would reconnect with old friends from previous trips and make countless new ones.

He was a familiar visitor at Black colleges and secondary schools, and he frequently lectured at Tuskegee Institute—twice at the invitation of its founder and president, Booker T. Washington—and at Fisk University. He maintained close contact with Black intellectuals and professors in both the North and South, and he ensured that they were well-aware of Bahá'í teachings. Shortly after his pilgrimage in 1911, he was recognized as one of the finest Bahá'í speakers in the country, with his earnest, powerful, and effective manner.

Louis always appreciated 'Abdu'l-Bahá's encouragement and support for his efforts to serve human oneness. 'Abdu'l-Bahá wrote to Louis, "I beseech God that He may graciously make thee the sign of His bounty amidst mankind, illumine thy face with the light of such blessings as are vouchsafed by the merciful Lord, single thee out for his love in this age which is distinguished among all the past ages and centuries."[3] 'Abdu'l-Bahá's call to Louis "inspired him to transcend the shortcomings of the society around him" and to demonstrate to younger Blacks and whites "how to overcome racial barriers."[4]

Of course, Louis was not alone among African Americans in accepting the teachings of Bahá'u'lláh. While every individual seeker has a unique spiritual experience in recognizing Bahá'u'lláh, the Bahá'í belief in the oneness of humanity is a reminder that we are all God's children and are equal in His eyes. Richard Thomas has written, "Bahá'u'lláh's teachings emphasizing the oneness of the human family . . . had a special appeal to African-Americans . . . Due to the long experience with White racial discrimination at the hands of State and Church, many African-Americans were attracted by the spirit of universality reflected in the words of Bahá'u'lláh from their first exposure."[5]

Bahá'í teachings gave him a new spiritual orientation. It reconciled "racial pride with the idea of human brotherhood."[6] The spiritual character of his service would not only help remove prejudice in America but throughout the world.

Without any doubt, Louis understood that since racial prejudice had become deeply rooted over many centuries into the fabric of American society, it would take time, tremendous perseverance, and effort to remove it. He had learned that Bahá'í teachings could help people find freedom from all forms of prejudice, if they wished.

Louis' love and gratitude to 'Abdu'l-Bahá constantly motivated him, and he followed His guidance and directions as best he could. Another guiding light was his love and gratitude to Shoghi Effendi. He also later obeyed his guidance and instructions to the best of his ability. Louis felt a personal connection with both leaders and a commitment to help implement programs of action they set. His attention to their directions underscored his accomplishments.

Within the Bahá'í community, 'Abdu'l-Bahá and Shoghi Effendi addressed some unease that some white Bahá'ís had about accepting Blacks as equals, and they reminded the Bahá'í world of the many spiritual qualities and characteristics Blacks possessed. 'Abdu'l-Bahá once remarked, "I had a servant who was black; his name was Isfandíyár. If a perfect man could be found in the world, that man was Isfandíyár. He was the essence of love, radiant with sanctity and perfection, luminous with light. Whenever I think of Isfandíyár, I am moved to tears, although he passed away fifty years ago. He was the faithful servant of Bahá'u'lláh and was entrusted with His secrets."[7]

Shoghi Effendi wrote, "The qualities of heart so richly possessed by the Negro are much needed in the world today—their great capacity for faith, their loyalty, and devotion to their religion when once they believe, their purity of heart, God has richly endowed them, and their contribution to the Cause is much needed."[8] Other spiritual qualities which impressed him were, as indicated by Rúḥíyyih Khánum, Shoghi Effendi's wife, "'humility,'" "'kindness,'" "'friendliness,'" "'courtesy,'" and "'hospitableness.'"[9]

Although they were in sharp contrast to views many whites held of Black people, these descriptions undoubtedly removed some misunderstandings. Louis served as the secretary of the Race Amity Committee, a committee appointed by the National Spiritual Assembly to stimulate local racial amity efforts.[10] In 1934, the committee attempted to increase understanding within the predominantly white Bahá'í community in which fixed silences and biased assumptions about race prevailed. The committee listed some of the following positive attributes of the Black community: "The amazing progress of the colored people . . . their increasing group consciousness and solidarity . . . their literature, art, scientific knowledge, collective enterprise; their keen sense of humor, cheerfulness under difficulties, stoical endurance of the economic depression; their ability when given a chance to measure up to the standards of other Americans; their native and cultivated graces which lend a fascination to their social life."[11] The committee also highlighted other spiritual qualities that have promoted this progress: ". . . their [African-Americans] faith in God and adherence to religion despite the largely prevalent agnosticism of the day; their conciliatory spirit; these and other qualities indicate powers which under divine guidance may yet, we trust, make a very considerable contribution to the world's net aggregate of service and universal progress."[12]

In this connection, Louis had learned that Bahá'u'lláh's teachings for the spiritual regeneration of humanity enabled everyone to have a heart for the unity of mankind, if they wished to strive for it, and he was keenly aware of the importance of initiating and maintaining contacts within the large and diverse American Black community. In July of 1909, he arranged a series of presentations of Bahá'í teachings to several large meetings of the Bethel Literary and Historical Association, of which he was president. It was the oldest and leading Black organization in Washington, DC. One lecture was on "'The Race Question from the Standpoint of the Bahai Revelation.'"[13]

The opportunities for Louis to be with 'Abdu'l-Bahá in 1911 during his pilgrimage,[14] and again in 1912 during 'Abdu'l-Bahá's epic visit to the United States,[15] provided precious moments for Louis to learn from 'Abdu'l-Bahá about how to serve humanity. As described by Venters, Louis' "series of profound encounters with 'Abdu'l-Bahá strengthened [his] bond with the center of the faith and cemented him in his life's work of promoting interracial unity."[16] He was also likely inspired by such Bahá'í teachings as these: "Bahá'u'lláh has drawn the circle of unity, He has made a design for the uniting of all the peoples, and for the gathering of them all under the shelter of the tent of universal unity."[17] Such teachings enabled him to understand the implications of this "design" and to urgently contribute to efforts by the American believers to implement it.

To help spread Bahá'u'lláh's vision of oneness, Louis visited forty-six states in the United States, and he conveyed to as many people as possible the Bahá'í approach to racial unity.[18] He spoke to thousands of individuals, hundreds of organizations, church congregations, student bodies, civic bodies, and teachers' associations about racial harmony and its link with human oneness. He also took the Bahá'í message to ten countries in two hemispheres and helped advance a new vision of racial unity with people from all strata of society, including the educated and the unlettered. Additionally, he formed study classes for advancing knowledge of the Bahá'í teachings around the country for those who were interested.

Louis with children at Green Acre in Eliot, Maine, in 1929. (US Bahá'í National Archives)

Children loved Louis, and whether traveling or at home, he worked to create interracial children's classes. For example, when he and his wife Louisa were living at Green Acre (in Eliot, Maine), he sometimes organized children's classes there. Later, the Louis Gregory Children's Class was established in 1970 there in his honor.[19] One participant in the classes recounted some of the spiritual qualities she had observed in Louis when she was eight years old. When they walked together one evening after a Bahá'í meeting, she recounted, "The night was dark and so was Mr. Gregory. . . . I looked up at him. My gaze was held for a moment on the beauty and peace of his face, but most of all, it was the shimmering radiance that was so remarkable, that seemed to be a part of him. I was amazed that in such a darkness . . . there could be so much light. I was unable to take my eyes off of his face."[20]

In Louis' day, church membership was often an important indicator of respectability and social standing within Black communities. When Louis became a Bahá'í, some of Louis' friends in Washington, DC, thought he'd made a wrong spiritual choice, and others thought he had committed professional suicide. He recalled, "'By far the majority of my friends thought I had become mentally unbalanced.'" He also recalled, "'One of my old teachers, a professor of international law and a very affectionate friend, almost wept over my departure from orthodoxy [the Christian faith].'" Others, he recounted, warned that "'I was blasting all hopes of a career.'"[21]

And that wasn't all the pity and criticism he got for quietly, calmly, and respectfully promoting racial equality based on Bahá'í teachings. A popular Black newspaper rebuked him, even though before he became a Bahá'í, it had favorably publicized his activities and opinions.

Louis recounted, "'The *Washington Bee*, a well-known colored newspaper, on one occasion gave me two columns of ridicule.'"[22] The columns were published in January and June 1911. In the first, the writer praised Louis as "'one of the most studious, pious and gentlemanly young men in Washington.'" The writer attributed Louis' "'aberrant behavior [becoming a Bahá'í] to the fact that he was not yet married.'" He pronounced that Louis had erred in deciding "'to take up with some mummified, prehistoric pinch-hitter like Buddha or Confucius or a minor leaguer like Baha . . .'" He stated, "'I never could see anything in conditions in India and the Orient to make their religion, or any religion that came from such environments, appeal to me.'"[23] The second column, by the same writer, ridiculed the Bahá'í Faith as one of a number of "'Oriental get-rich-quick creeds'" attracting "'high-brows and faddist,'" who were no longer satisfied with traditional Protestantism.[24]

Louis set the record straight. Later that year, in November 1911, the *Washington Bee* published a front-page article he wrote. In the article, Louis outlined the Bahá'í Faith's teachings, objectives, and history, and he emphasized the Faith's harmony with Christianity. He wrote. "'The Revelation of Bahá'[u]'lláh is not a new Religion. It is rather a renewal of the Spirit of Religion. It comes to antagonize no existing church, sect, or religion, but rather to unite all.'"[25]

Louis weathered the storm of criticism, and he did not slow down his Bahá'í activities. "[H]e saw even the opposition to his having become a Bahá'í as a partly constructive thing,"[26] as "'there were always some who were willing to investigate and the opposition seemed to promote inquiry.'"[27]

The people who criticized him couldn't see that he had found in the Bahá'í teachings what he felt was his true self. The teachings freed him from enslavement of any kind, and they anchored him to something larger than himself, larger than his family and his race. They helped him make sense of himself in a chaotic world of color he had found confusing and overwhelming. He didn't feel lost, small, or bereft, nor did he put aside his undiminished concern for racial equality and social justice, nor did he lose touch with individuals and groups working for social progress in their own way.

Another action he took for change after becoming a Bahá'í was to confront racial prejudice in the partially segregated, mostly white, Washington, DC Bahá'í community. Some white members still resisted the spiritual and social implications of the Bahá'í teachings on the oneness of the human race. Many hesitated to hold interracial meetings, especially in white homes, out of concern for what people would say.[28] Racial intermingling in homes, public places, and religious congregations was not common in the city, and in the Bahá'í community, the principles of oneness and racial equality the Hannens lived by were not accepted by all white Bahá'ís.

Louis wrote the Hannens, "'As soon as I became a believer and began to teach, . . . my colored friends got on my back and began to press me with troublous questions.'" Here are the three questions they asked: "'If this were a New religion which stood for unity, why were its devotees divided? Why did they not meet altogether in one place? Were the Bahá'ís not full of prejudice like other people?'"[29]

It was as if his friends were asking him, "What are you going to do, Louis?" His letter to the Hannens continued, "'If you are not busy on Saturday evening, I want to have a talk with you and have a clear understanding in regard to the attitude of the local assembly [the local community] toward the colored believers. It is with sincere regret that I find it necessary to bring this matter up, and only because some impressions are going abroad which I fear will injure our Cause both among the white and colored.'" He went on to explain, "'I have nothing to complain of that is of a personal nature. But 'Abdu'l-Bahá has said that slight differences now may be great differences hereafter. And for this reason I do not wish the awful responsibility of being the cause or occasion of any schism to rest upon my shoulders.'"[30]

Had he crossed the lines of propriety? It seems at the time that no one in his community talked openly about race. It may have been considered rude. Writing that letter was a first step toward change, and the tone of Louis' letter was respectful, candid, and courteous. But the prejudice within his Bahá'í community had placed "[Louis] in an embarrassing position"[31] and was undermining his credibility with his Black friends.[32]

Louis pointed out the divisive practice because he was worried that growing public awareness of it would "'injure our Cause both among the white and colored.'"[33] Apparently some in his community didn't fully appreciate why Black members detested segregation. Louis knew that wherever it was practiced, segregation created divisions in a community, and that these divisions in the DC Bahá'í community would only fester if the issue of segregation was not addressed.

Later, he expressed how segregation struck at his heart. In 1932, in his capacity as secretary of the National Bahá'í Committee for Racial Amity, he wrote a letter to the Local Spiritual Assembly of Detroit regarding the dangers of even appearing to stand for segregation. He stated, "'The intelligentsia of the colored race, . . . will welcome any cooperative, interracial efforts on the part of the Baha'is and other liberal movements. . . . But they will fight to the last ditch any organization that proposes to segregate them. . . . For the Cause of Baha'u'llah to be committed to a different stand will put it under fire both of the colored and liberal whites . . . An interracial study class will do good. But a segregated study class is fore-doomed to failure, I fear.'"[34] He knew that opposing segregation, especially when it occurred within a religious organization, was deeply rooted in Black history in America. In 1792, while at worship at St. George's Methodist Episcopal Church (Philadelphia), Richard Allen, Absalom Jones, and others had sat for worship with white worshipers, and they had sat down with them for communion. However, the Black congregants were pulled up and were told they couldn't sit down with or take communion with white congregation members. They had to sit against the wall, in the gallery, and on the balcony. At that point, Richard Allen and most of the church's Black members walked out. Stricken with painful humiliation, they resolved they would never return to a segregated worship. The segregation was a sign of the hypocrisy of some white churches, where whites believed Blacks, even within the church, were spiritually and socially inferior. Allen and the others couldn't bear the contempt in God's house anymore. Black worshippers had been rendered inconsequential, invisible, and unwelcomed. In 1793, they formed the Bethel African Methodist Episcopal Church. It was America's first independent Black religious denomination.[35]

Despite the prejudice he had seen in his Bahá'í community, Louis remained hopeful. According to Louis Venters, Louis believed "that if even a handful of white Bahá'ís . . . were willing to overcome their prejudices and to associate intimately with blacks, the rest would follow."[36]

The Hannens informed Louis that "'the matter [the three questions Louis referred to earlier in the chapter] had never come up'" in the community.[37] Undoubtedly, the contradiction between the Bahá'í teachings and the racially biased practices in the DC Bahá'í community had become troubling for some white Bahá'ís even before Louis had sent his letter. But when would the practice of segregation become unbearable? The Hannens arranged for him to consult with "the Working Committee," an elected, administrative body of the local community. No record exists of that meeting, but no immediate steps were taken to begin regular integrated meetings that year.[38]

This lack of a response didn't diminish Louis' desire to share Bahá'í teachings with others, nor did it dampen his spirit. After all, the Bahá'í Faith was his Faith, too, and he remained confident that its teachings would help resolve racial prejudice within his community and beyond.

In 1910, the Washington, DC Bahá'í community held its first interracial meeting.[39] In 1911, Louis was elected to its Working Committee.[40] He had now become the first person of African descent to serve on a Bahá'í administrative body in the United States.[41] One year later, in April 1912, at the National Convention of the Bahá'í Temple Unity (a body formed to promote the construction of the Bahá'í House of Worship), he was elected to that organization's executive board.[42] In 1922, the Bahá'í Temple Unity was renamed the National Spiritual Assembly of the Bahá'is of the United States.[43]

Louis served on the National Spiritual Assembly of the Bahá'ís of the United States and Canada for a total of fourteen years, and he was the only African American to serve on that body until 1946.[44] It was the beginning of decades of service on Bahá'í institutions in the American Bahá'í community.

5

PILGRIMAGE

On March 25, 1911, at 'Abdu'l-Bahá's invitation, Louis sailed from New York for his Bahá'í pilgrimage. The trip was his first overseas, and it was a tremendous milestone in his life for an advancing appreciation of the interrelationship between Blacks and whites in America and the acceptance of the principle of human oneness by peoples throughout the world. The Master was currently staying at His temporary residence in Alexandria, Egypt,[1] to regain His health, which had suffered during forty years of confinement. He was receiving pilgrims en route to Palestine (Israel), where they would visit the Shrine of Bahá'u'lláh and the Shrine of the Báb, Bahá'u'lláh's Forerunner.[2]

Undoubtedly, Louis' commitment to the principle of human oneness was rooted in his close relationship with 'Abdu'l-Bahá, the Exemplar of Bahá'í ideals. Morrison writes, "From the start 'Abdu'l-Bahá had given Louis Greogry not only the goal but the encouragement he needed in order to achieve it."[3] Louis had an instinctive and heartfelt aspiration to begin his pilgrimage.

'Abdu'l-Bahá wrote of meeting Louis, "'Mr. Gregory arrived with the utmost love and spirituality,'" and He envisioned he "'shall progress'" in his spiritual growth and his service to the oneness of humanity.

During his time with Him, 'Abdu'l-Bahá answered Louis' questions and encouraged him to persevere in his service for racial unity.[4]

During Louis' nearly two weeks in Egypt, 'Abdu'l-Bahá showered him with affection. Gayle Morrison, Louis' biographer, has also observed, "He crossed in freedom the ocean that his forebears had traversed in chains. Moreover, he landed on the African continent with a new ethnic awareness."[5] Of his arrival on African soil on April 4, 1911, Louis noted, "'We land[ed] at Alger [Algeria], and for the first time I set foot on the shore of Africa, my ancient Fatherland.'"[6]

Gayle Morrison writes that, from the crossing of the Atlantic and his arrival on African soil, Louis realized "that blacks had made a unique adaptation to America precisely because their ties with Africa had been so ruthlessly cut."[7] Louis wrote, "'. . . no other American group . . . is more American.'"[8] After his voyage, he was strengthened in his conviction that "blacks belonged in America" and that "their rightful presence and full integration in every aspect of society would eventually be recognized even by extremists of both races."[9]

In Egypt, with a new "ethnic awareness,"[10] Louis asked 'Abdu'l-Bahá's "'special consideration'" for "'the African tribes.'"[11] 'Abdu'l-Bahá reportedly told him, "'You must be a leader to them. Guide them to the truth.'"[12] The Master is also reported to have, according to Louis Venters, "extolled the ancient black civilizations of Egypt and Ethiopia."[13]

Louis knew that Westerners often considered Africa to be "a continent outside of history."[14] Prejudice against dark-skinned people was generally worldwide. For instance, after landing in 1492 in what is now known as the nation of Haiti, Christopher Columbus wrote in his diary, "'They are a people very poor in everything. . . . they have no language. . . ." It was also observed that "[t]hey lacked weapons, they lacked tools. . . . they lacked even faith. . . ." He even proclaimed that: "They . . . have no religion.'"[15]

Later Columbus emphasized that the people had no "'ways and beliefs.'"[16] He saw every difference between the natives of Haiti and white Europeans as proof that the natives were "'infidels and savages who could not rightfully own anything.'"[17] Columbus was thus one of the first European explorers to establish false notions about indigenous peoples in "'the new world.'"[18] One can readily deduce, especially in the erroneous assumption that the peoples had no spiritual foundation, that these unfounded claims accelerated the self-serving notions of white superiority and the inferiority of dark-skinned people.

By contrast, the Bahá'í writings explain that indigenous peoples around the world have had, over the ages, great tribal, or primal, oral religions.[19] These religions spiritually uplifted and empowered their civilizations. As Houston Smith has explained in his book, *The World's Religions,* "The written world religions (those with written scriptures) now pretty much cover the world, but chronologically they form only the tip of the religious iceberg; for they span less than four thousand years as compared with the three million years or so of the religions that preceded them. During that immense time span, people had what is now largely referred to as 'primal religions'—*primal because they came first*—sometimes referred to as tribal, because its groupings were small, or oral, because writing was unknown to them. This mode of religiosity continues in Africa, Australia, Southwest Asia, the Pacific Islands, Siberia, and among the Indians of North and South America."[20]

The following is a portion of what the Bahá'í teachings reveal on this subject: "Thus there have been many holy Manifestations of God. One thousand years ago, two hundred thousand years ago, one million years ago the bounty of God was flowing, the radiance of God was shining, the dominion of God was existing."[21]

According to Mírzá Abu'l-Faḍl, a distinguished Bahá'í scholar, "'. . . even religions that appear to consist of idol-worship and are condemned as heathen were in fact originally true religions from God, the original pure teachings of which have been lost over the ages mainly through the action of religious leaders—[this] has clear implications for the encounter of the Bahá'í Faith with ethnic religions in Africa and other parts of the world.'"[22]

Louis was always proud of his African descent. According to Ruhe-Schoen, Louis "had a deep feeling for the African continent."[23]

While Louis was still in Egypt, 'Abdu'l-Bahá also inquired about the unity between the Black and white Bahá'ís in America. Even though Louis was painfully aware of the friction within the DC Bahá'í community, he answered diplomatically, "'there was not entire unity, but that there were earnest souls of both races who desired closer unity and hoped that He would point out to them the means of attaining it.'"[24] 'Abdu'l-Bahá is reported to have inquired further, "'Does this refer to the removal of hatreds and antagonisms on the part of one race, or of both races?'"[25] "'Both races,'" Louis answered.[26] 'Abdu'l-Bahá replied that it would be done.[27]

'Abdu'l-Bahá also shared with the pilgrims the Bahá'í approval of interracial marriage, and Gayle Morrison writes, "He addressed the sexual myths and fears at the heart of American racism."[28] He stated that Black and white Bahá'ís should not only be in unity but should intermarry, if they wished. He reportedly stated, "'All are equal. If you have any influence to get the races to intermarry, it will be very valuable.'"[29] He reportedly emphasized that interracial marriages would constitute "'a great service to the world of humanity.'"[30]

After his pilgrimage, when Louis was preparing to leave, the Master gently is reported to have addressed him in English: "'Speak to me, Mr. Gregory'"[31] He also reportedly said, "'My Gregory! My son!'"[32] At hearing these words, Louis felt "'a thrill of joy.'"[33]

'Abdu'l-Bahá reportedly suggested some means for achieving unity and harmony among the believers. He directed him, "'Go forth and speak of the Cause of God. Visit the friends. Gladden their hearts. You will be the means of Guidance to many souls. The Divine Bounties will be with you. You are always in my mind and heart.'"[34] Later, one of the Master's translators said to Louis, "'This morning 'Abdu'l-Bahá . . . told me to say to you: "Keep your face turned to the Kingdom and fear nothing!"'"[35]

'Abdu'l-Bahá had instructed Louis to "'lecture at Haifa.'"[36] Louis wondered how to do that since he would be surrounded by older, knowledgeable Bahá'ís. He easily made presentations at the Master's home about "the progress of the Cause in America and . . . racial conditions."[37]

At 'Abdu'l-Bahá's request, Louis visited Germany, Paris, and London on his way home to the United States after his pilgrimage to the Holy Land.[38] In letters both to believers in Germany and America, 'Abdu'l-Bahá expressed the high regard in which He held Louis. He mentioned that the pilgrimage had matured and strengthened him and wrote, "'Verily, he has much advanced in his journey. He received another life, and obtained another power. When he returned, Gregory was, quite another Gregory. He had become a new creation.'"[39]

Photo of Louis, date unknown. (US Bahá'í National Archives)

To one of the Washington Bahá'ís, 'Abdu'l-Bahá wrote, "'Mr. Gregory arrived with the utmost love and spirituality and returned with infinite happiness. He added to his faith and assurance and found firmness and steadfastness. Undoubtedly you shall see these things at the time of his arrival. It is my hope that he may become the cause of increasing the love of the friends.'"[40] In another letter, 'Abdu'l-Bahá suggested the kind of welcome the returning pilgrim should receive: "'Mr. Gregory . . . will return to America very soon, and you, the white people, should then honor and welcome this shining colored man in such a way that all the people will be astonished.'"[41]

The warm welcome described by 'Abdu'l-Bahá never took place. It may not have mattered to Louis, for he had discovered that, through visiting the Sacred Shrines and conversing with 'Abdu'l-Bahá, he had received a fresh inspiration and power to serve the oneness and wholeness of humanity. He hoped 'Abdu'l-Bahá would soon visit America.

6

A SPECIAL MARRIAGE ENCOURAGED BY 'ABDU'L-BAHÁ

'Abdu'l-Bahá arrived in New York on April 11, 1912, for his eight-month journey across America. According to Janet Ruhe-Schoen, during the Master's visit to the United States in 1912, Mr. Gregory received from Him "the structure and pattern for his life, and his importance in the Master-plan (so to speak!) would be further clarified."[1]

Gayle Morrison has observed that 'Abdu'l-Bahá's visit "indelibly marked the course of Bahá'í history in America."[2] He Himself reportedly proclaimed: "'It is my purpose to set forth the fundamental principles of the revelation and teachings of Baha 'Ullah. It will then become the duty of the Bahais of this country to give these principles unfoldment and application in the minds, hearts and lives of the people.'"[3] Morrison writes: "In statements to the general public and the press He emphasized that He sought to further the cause of unity and peace. Among the Bahá'ís He stressed that His ultimate purpose was to transform them spiritually, in order that they might help to bring about the oneness of mankind."[4] Janet

Ruhe-Schoen points out, "Oneness, particularly the oneness of the human race and its expression in racial amity" was the major focus of 'Abdu'l-Bahá's visit. She continues, "It was, indeed, the hallmark of His message to the world. As He saw it, realization of fundamental human oneness is the primary requisite for the establishment of real and lasting world peace."[5]

'Abdu'l-Bahá came with several attendants, secretaries, a translator, and six Western Bahá'ís. Among them was an English woman named Miss Louise Mathew.[6] She was christened Louisa Alice Maria, but for all her adult life, she preferred to be called Louise.[7] She had met 'Abdu'l-Bahá with radiant humility and joy for the first time in 1911 on her Bahá'í pilgrimage.[8] Louis had also been in this same pilgrim group in which 'Abdu'l-Bahá spoke about interracial marriage.[9] Louis often spoke and wrote about his pilgrim experiences, but neither he nor Louise could ever have imagined that meeting with 'Abdu'l-Bahá in the United States would transform their lives forever.

Louise had already achieved considerable accomplishments for the Faith. She was born in 1866 to an affluent, hardy British family of farmers, tradesmen, and businesspeople in southern England. She spent her childhood and teenage years living in London, and she recalled that she had "been out of orthodox thought on religion since [she] was sixteen."[10] From the time she was a teenager, she set out on a search for truth that would take her into her forties before she found and accepted the Bahá'í teachings.[11]

Her father, Mr. Michael Mathew, died in March, 1909. From a humble beginning, he had built up his own company in the egg-importing and grocery business, and he had made provisions for each of his surviving eleven children to receive an equal share of income from his considerable investments.[12]

After her father's passing, Louise received regular payments of interest on her inheritance for the rest of her life, and this financial arrangement enabled her to live with a degree of independence that yielded remarkable results. In or around 1908, she met a group of Bahá'ís in Paris, where she had been investigating the Faith's teachings.[13] 'Abdu'l-Bahá's letters comforted and guided her, and in December of 1909, she wrote to Him and declared her faith in Bahá'u'lláh. From that point forward, she developed a deep love and understanding of the Bahá'í teachings. She fully embraced the Bahá'í Faith, and, according to Ruhe-Schoen, "wanted nothing more than to dedicate her life to it."[14]

In letters to her, 'Abdu'l-Bahá expressed His "'extreme love and affection'" for her. He commended her "'kindness to the children of the poor.'" In another letter, He commended "'the devotion'" of her heart and the "'purity'" of her "'soul.'" He described her as a "'daughter of the Kingdom.'"[15] He also told her, "'I am your Father, you are my daughter.'"[16]

Louise was an intelligent, caring woman who treated everyone with respect. She pursued a course of academic studies, which was unusual for a woman in her day. She attended Royal Holloway College, St. George's Training College in Edinburgh, and Edinburgh University, and she completed training to become a teacher. Additionally, she had private tutoring in music, voice, French, and German. She was able to show remarkable perseverance in the face of contemporary society's denigration of the importance of education for women.[17]

When Louise arrived with 'Abdu'l-Bahá in America, she had no thought of marriage.[18] Neither did Louis.[19] However, Louise understood from an unexpected conversation with 'Abdu'l-Bahá in Chicago that He wished her and Louis to marry. Then she related, "'Curiously enough after this love began to grow in my heart & the desire for the marriage whereas before I only liked Mr. Gregory as a friend.'"[20]

During her conversation with Him, she asked 'Abdu'l-Bahá if He wanted her and Louis to marry. He reportedly said "'"yes"'" and asked her, "'"Do you love him, would you marry him if he asked you?"'" She replied, "'"Yes."'" Then He said, "'"if he loves you he will ask you."'" Later, He told Louis, "'"I would be very pleased if you and Miss Mathew were to marry."'" It was an utter surprise. Louis was speechless. "'"What is the matter?"'" 'Abdu'l-Bahá inquired,

"'"Don't you love her?"'" "'"Yes as a friend,"'" Louis responded. 'Abdu'l-Bahá replied, "'"Well think of it & let me know; . . . marriage is not an ordinance & need not be obeyed, but it would give me much pleasure if you & Miss Mathew were to marry."'"[21]

Louis walked around Chicago for hours pondering the suggestion. On the one hand, he was proud of being an African American. On the other hand, even though he struggled against racial prejudice day after day, he had no fear of marrying outside his race. He was also very fond of Louise.[22]

Louis knew he could reject the suggestion and that others had rejected 'Abdu'l-Bahá's matchmaking suggestions in the past.[23] Recognizing their love for one another and the wisdom of 'Abdu'l-Bahá, he and Louise decided to marry. Louis expressed his love in such words as these: "'May God cement our souls together and make us richer by the Divine outpouring of His Spirit of Love.'"[24]

Louis and Louise were married on September 27, 1912, in New York City. Here are some sentiments in the prayer 'Abdu'l-Bahá revealed for their union: "O Lord! Assist them . . . and destine for them every good through Thy bounty and grace. . . . Cause them to become the signs of harmony and unity until the end of time."[25]

'Abdu'l-Bahá lauded their union and "never failed to assure them of His support."[26] He wrote to them, "'Continually do I remember you. I beg of God that through you good fellow-ship may be obtained between the white and the black for you are an introduction to the accomplishment.'"[27]

Their marriage was the first interracial marriage between a Black and a white Bahá'í. Shoghi Effendi referred to it as "the exemplary act He ('Abdu'l-Bahá) performed by uniting in wedlock two of His followers of different nationalities, one of the white, the other of the Negro race."[28] According to Mr. Gregory's biographer, Gayle Morrison, "Their union served as a perpetual reminder of the Bahá'í position on the oneness of humankind."[29]

Louis Gregory and Louise Mathew were committed to their love for each other. Janet Ruhe-Schoen has written, "They were proud of their marriage, their chosen Faith, and each other."[30] She con-

Louis and Louise Gregory, 1913. (US Bahá'í National Archives)

tinues by writing that Louis "always" had his wife's "unconditional support."[31] They grew together spiritually in wonderful harmony. Louis and Louise were equally devoted to the Cause, and Louise "was proud of Louis's achievements and supported him in every way she could."[32] Likewise, Louis was proud of her achievements and fully supported her in her endeavors.[33]

The issue of their separation from one another was a constant factor in their lives. In this connection, Louis once observed, "'It is our hope that our enforced separation along the lines of service to the Divine Cause will mercifully bring to us eternal reunion in the worlds of God.'"[34] As the years passed, their shared goals in life continued to bind the Gregorys together. Louis observed in 1950 that Louise's "'fine cooperation in teaching service has been a tower of strength to me.'"[35]

Despite the great distances that kept them apart, Louise wrote to her husband "as a woman deeply in love, intent on the well-being of her husband, and acutely conscious of the miles between them."[36] In 1934, when Louise was in Europe, she "expressed her awareness of distance in poignant terms."[37] She wrote, "'I do wonder how you are getting on & where you are my sweet boy . . .'"[38] Louis often made his love for Louise and his appreciation for her loving support plain. He wrote, "'I am grateful to God that through Divine Favor the way is opened to this unworthy servant. My dear little wife, the Flame of whose spiritual love is aglow . . .'"[39]

At this time in the United States and elsewhere, "scientific" theories of white superiority, Black inferiority, and the harmful effects of racial intermarriage abounded.[40] Interracial marriage was also a criminal offense in most American states. It would be over fifty years before the US Supreme Court ruled that state laws prohibiting interracial marriage were unconstitutional.[41]

Louis and Louise's marriage was also difficult for some Black and white Bahá'ís to accept. Louis bore, as he described them, "'The vile reproaches of people of both races.'"[42] All their married lives, he said, he suffered criticism that descended on him "'for a step which I have never regretted.'"[43] "Outside the small circle of their friends," according to Gayle Morrison, "the Gregorys' actions were subjected continually to scrutiny and criticism."[44] As Janet Rose points out, "In marrying Louis she [Louise] had embraced the many problems associated in those days with marrying a man of different race: the problem of finding a place to live where a mixed race couple was accepted, and no doubt facing the hardship of a certain amount of shunning from people who disliked their interracial marriage for one reason or another."[45]

According to Ruhe-Schoen, "Despite intense opposition to intermarriage in both white and black communities, there was some support for it, usually because of belief in the principle of oneness . . ."[46] Louis clearly demonstrated his commitment to Bahá'í teachings of interracial marriage by action.

Louis and Louise did find support from some in the Bahá'í community, however. Below are excerpts from a letter to 'Abdul-Bahá in March 1914 written by Coralie Franklin Cook, a Black Bahá'í of Washington, DC, expressing her full support for interracial marriage. Coralie Franklin Cook was a professor at Howard University and served on the Racial Amity Committee with Louis.[47] She used principles of the Bahá'í Faith as a means of cultivating more open attitudes towards the Faith's teachings.[48] She, along with her husband George, who held the position of Professor of Commercial and International Law at Howard University, became a Bahá'í in 1913.[49] In 1914, she shared with 'Abdul-Bahá that she and other believers "'do not make the mistake of supposing that 'Abdul-Bahá does not understand far more about this matter than any believer can possibly show him, but we do feel it fitting to put on record and into your hands certain facts as expressing the attitude of the colored people themselves concerning race prejudice.'"[50]

In the same letter to 'Abdu'l-Bahá, Mrs. Cook also wrote, "'No phase of the color question excites so much rancor and misrepresentation as the one of mixed marriage. It is constantly made use of by all classes of whites . . . and now includes some so-called Bahá'ís to arouse passion and strife . . . If the whole truth were told, it must be said that many colored people are as strongly opposed to inter-racial marriage as the whites . . . So far as the matter of amalgamation goes here in the United States, it is settled past undoing. 250 years of domestic slavery with the female slave at the command of her master has bequeathed to the country hundreds, yes thousands, of mixed bloods . . . This mixing of the two Races we are told is biologically unfit, will degrade posterity and vitiate the noble Saxon blood . . .

Intelligent colored people have no craving for intermarriage, nor do they inveigh against it, they take the position that it is a question for the two parties concerned to settle for themselves . . .'"[51]

Despite the opposition to their marriage from some inside the Bahá'í community, the Gregorys' love for each other, their faith, their wonderful, and caring service together for racial equality saw them through every difficulty. Louise once wrote to a prominent member of the Washington, DC Bahá'í community: "'My husband and I are very truly one in all essential things. . . .'"[52] Some Bahá'ís doubted that Louis and Louise's union could last in a segregated society. However, the marriage lasted until their deaths close to four decades later. Throughout this period, Louis and Louise became the ultimate Bahá'í symbol of racial unity, love, and friendship.[53]

Eight years after their marriage in 1920, Louise received a Tablet from 'Abdu'l-Bahá. In addition to extolling her husband's spiritual station, He again blessed their marriage and commended both for serving human oneness together. He wrote, "'To the dear maid-servant of God, Mrs. Louise Gregory: Unto her be the Glory of God, the Most Glorious. HE IS GOD! O thou revered wife of his honour, Gregory! Do thou consider what a bounty God hath bestowed upon thee in giving thee a husband as Mr. Gregory, who is the essence of the love of God and is a symbol of guidance! How luminous is the face of this person! His character is (like unto) a rose-garden. He is always busy, together with thee, in service of the Kingdom. Ye are always serving together . . . with all your power, raising the Call of God.'"[54]

As Janet Fleming Rose has observed, "For the rest of her [Louise's] life she cherished two guiding lights which motivated her constantly. One was her love and gratitude to 'Abdu'l-Bahá with Whom she felt a personal connection. This love flowered into her lifelong service to the Cause of Bahá'u'lláh despite manifold difficulties. The other was her love for Louis and their marriage which were both directly attributable to 'Abdu'l-Bahá."[55]

7

COMPELLING LESSONS FROM 'ABDU'L-BAHÁ ABOUT ONENESS

During 'Abdu'l-Bahá's memorable visit with Bahá'ís in Washington, DC, the Master—Who had bold, tender, and practical ways of offering insight for the heart—presented a most compelling lesson on the oneness of humanity. Indeed, Louis' "active concern for the advancement of black people . . . and his special interest in unity between blacks and whites, the mission given him by 'Abdu'l-Bahá, never narrowed his vision or limited his audiences. Rather, oneness served as a key to his understanding all the various elements of a new world order and to his genuine concern for all oppressed people."[1]

On April 23, 1912, with Louis at his side, 'Abdu'l-Bahá challenged the practice of social segregation in Washington, DC. He had been invited to attend a luncheon and a reception at the home of the *charge d'affaires* of the Persian Legation, Mírzá Ali-Kuli Khan, who was also a Bahá'í. Gayle Morrison writes that "[a]bout nineteen guests were present."[2] Louis recalls that some were "'very prominent in the social and political life of Washington.'"[3] Gayle Morrison has also written, "About an hour before the luncheon 'Abdu'l-Bahá had sent word to Louis to come to the Khans' for an interview."[4] Harlan

Ober recounts, "'Louis arrived at the appointed time, and the conference went on and on . . . 'Abdu'l-Bahá seemed to want to prolong it.'"[5] Gayle Morrison has further noted, "Finally [the] luncheon was announced, and, as 'Abdu'l-Bahá led the invited guests to the dining room, . . . Mr. Gregory waited for the chance to leave the house unobtrusively."[6] Harlan Ober recalls:

> All were seated when suddenly 'Abdu'l-Bahá stood up, looked all around, and then said to Mírzá Khan, "Where is Mr. Gregory? Bring Mr. Gregory!" There was nothing for Mírzá Khan to do but find Mr. Gregory. . . . Finally Mr. Gregory came into the room with Mírzá Khan. 'Abdu'l-Bahá, Who was really the Host (as He was wherever He was), had by this time, rearranged the place settings and made room for Mr. Gregory, giving him the seat of honor at His right. He stated He was very pleased to have Mr. Gregory there, and then, in the most natural way as if nothing unusual had happened, proceeded to give a talk on the oneness of mankind.[7]

Of the lesson 'Abdu'l-Bahá taught on that occasion, Louis himself recalled, "'Abdul-Bahá made everyone feel perfectly at ease by His genial humor, wisdom, and outpouring of love.'"[8] With love and respect for Louis, 'Abdu'l-Bahá demonstrated Bahá'u'lláh's teachings on race relations and challenged the practice of social segregation. By so casually rearranging the place settings laid according to the strict demands of Washington protocol, He swept aside both segregation by race and categorization by social rank. Gayle Morrison remarks, "Gently, yet unmistakably, 'Abdu'l-Bahá had assaulted the customs of a city."[9]

So Louis was invited to that luncheon by its new "Host," Who easily discerned the direction and the possibilities of events. 'Abdu'l-Bahá sat Louis next to Him, and it is possible that He wanted it known that in His own seating arrangements, Louis deserved to be at the head of the table. If this were so, maybe it was because of

Louis and Ali Kuli Khan, undated photo.
(US Bahá’í National Archives)

Louis' character, his unwavering belief in the oneness of humanity, and his service to it in that segregated city and beyond.

'Abdu'l-Bahá's subtle but firm approach to challenging the ingrained racial prejudice in the DC Bahá'í community on this occasion served as an inspiration to Louis for confronting racial prejudice. Using various approaches in both private and public meetings, 'Abdu'l-Bahá raised the call of the oneness of humanity and challenged others to do the same.

Louis arranged for 'Abdu'l-Bahá to give a talk, attended by a biracial audience of about sixteen hundred people, at Howard University, the premiere Black university in the country at that time.[10]

The US Congress chartered Howard University in 1867. It was founded that year by General Oliver Otis Howard, a Civil War hero and commissioner of the Freedmen's Bureau to provide higher education for African Americans. The Howard University School of Law is one of the oldest law schools in the country and the oldest historically Black law school in the United States. It was established in 1869 to provide legal education for Americans who were traditionally excluded from the profession, particularly African Americans.[11]

This occasion of 'Abdu'l-Bahá's presentation demonstrated His ability to lovingly confront the racial prejudice of American society. Louis regarded it as "'perhaps the most powerful and impressive of all His utterances on race relations'" during His visit.[12] He wrote:

> The Master on this occasion went to the heart of the race problem. It was a talk which combined simplicity, beautiful imagery, noble idealism and practical applications with a spiritual atmosphere which raised His hearers to a pitch of joyous enthusiasm. The applause which followed was so long continued that this marvelous speaker felt moved to speak briefly a second time, assuring that a time would eventually come when all differences [between the races] would fade. It appeared to be His wish that the problem of the races in America should be worked out along lines stated in this address and in view of its extreme importance it should not only be read but studied.[13]

Here are extracts from the talk:

> I see here a gathering of the servants of God. I see white and black sitting together. There are no whites and blacks before God. All colors are one, and that is the color of servitude to God. . . . The heart is important. If the heart is pure, white or black or any color makes no difference. God does not look at colors; He looks at the hearts. He whose heart is pure is better. He whose character is better is more pleasing. . . . In the realm of existence colors are of no importance. . . . The world of humanity . . . is like a garden, and humankind are like the many-colored flowers. . . . I am very happy that white and black have gathered together in this meeting. I hope this coming together and harmony reaches such a degree that no distinctions shall remain between them, and they shall be together in the utmost harmony and love. But I wish to say one thing in order that the blacks may become grateful to the whites and the whites become loving toward the blacks. If you go to Africa and see the blacks of Africa, you will realize how much progress you have made. . . . The first proclamation of emancipation for the blacks was made by the whites of America. . . . Then it spread to other places. The blacks of Africa were in complete bondage, but your emancipation led to their freedom also—that is, the European states emulated the Americans, and the emancipation proclamation became universal. . . . Were it not for this effort, universal emancipation would not have been proclaimed. . . . Strive jointly to make extraordinary progress and mix together completely. . . . I pray that you attain to such a degree of good character and behavior that the names of black and white shall vanish. All shall be called human, ... I hope that you attain to such a high degree—and this is impossible except through love. You must try to create love between yourselves; . . . . Differences between black and white will be completely obliterated; indeed, ethnic and national differences will all disappear. . . . [T]hank God that this meeting is com-

> posed of people of both races and that both are gathered in perfect love and harmony. I hope this becomes the example of universal harmony and love until no title remains except that of humanity. Such a title demonstrates the perfection of the human world and is the cause of eternal glory and human happiness. I pray that you be with one another in utmost harmony and love and strive to enable each other to live in comfort.[14]

Morrison writes that "'Abdu'l-Bahá's addresses to large gatherings of influential blacks in Washington, DC and Chicago . . . permanently established the Bahá'í Faith in the consciousness of black America. The new religion had been almost unknown among blacks until Louis became a Bahá'í. Through his efforts, it was by 1912 no longer completely obscure . . . 'Abdu'l-Bahá had greatly extended the process of acquainting black Americans with the teachings of Bahá'u'lláh."[15]

Another of 'Abdu'l-Bahá's talks stressed, even more directly, the importance of eliminating racial prejudice. The Master reportedly said, "'It is prejudice that destroys the world. Every enmity, war, misunderstanding and suffering that has ever occurred in this world has been from either religious, patriotic, racial or political prejudice.'"[16]

According to Gayle Morrison, Louis "listened carefully, as he always had, absorbing not only 'Abdu'l-Bahá's words but His rapport with the audience."[17] She writes, "From 'Abdu'l-Bahá's example, Mr. Gregory learned to become familiar with the goals and concerns of each audience and to 'find the point of contact.'"[18] She continues:

> He also learned that to find the point of contact one did not have to tell an audience what it wanted to hear or to commiserate over its problems. Indeed, 'Abdu'l-Bahá's addresses both to blacks and to Jews in America never dwelled on their misfortunes. Although He, too, had known suffering at the hands of the unjust . . . in His public talks to minority groups He did not go over the common ground of persecution . . .

> Rather than intensify a natural preoccupation with oppression, 'Abdu'l-Bahá sought to foster confidence in the power to effect change. For blacks, whose color He described with approbation, this meant, on the one hand, development of a sense of one's own beauty and worth, and, on the other hand, reinforcement of the good qualities of whites through praise and appreciation. It also meant taking a larger view, broadening one's perspectives both historically and internationally.[19]

Morrison makes other observations as well regarding the Master's talks:

> . . . in His public talks in America 'Abdu'l-Bahá . . . preferred, as He Himself explained, not to "sadden" His audiences. He did not dwell on the deficiencies of the present order. Instead, He encouraged his listeners, pointing out "the oases rather than the deserts of their environments," as Louis Gregory once observed. "'Abdu'l-Bahá envisioned a new sociology for the world in general and America in particular."
>
> His public themes did not spring . . . from unfamiliarity with or disregard for the terrible obstacles blacks faced in their efforts to achieve equality in America. Rather, He sought to nurture the positive attitudes among blacks that would stave off desperation, hopelessness, growing hatred, and the ultimate disaster of racial warfare . . .[20]

She further observes:

> Louis Gregory heard both the encouragement to constructive action in 'Abdu'l-Bahá's speeches and His private warnings about racial violence. He readily understood the personal implication of 'Abdu'l-Bahá's assertion that brotherhood "is not possible without will and effort on the part of each" of the races . . . Mr. Gregory believed that the teachings of Bahá'u'lláh had stripped away all traces of anger and hatred from his own

> heart. He knew that these emotions, however well justified, simply intensify oppression, whereas positive attitudes erode its foundations. As he once told an audience, "It is only by co-operation, mutual appreciation, and good will that we can get anywhere in the solution of these problems that vex us. If this room were filled with darkness we could not remove that darkness by intensifying the darkness, nor can we remove discord from the face of the earth by increasing discord."[21]

Louis once wrote, "'. . . one marvels at the Divine Wisdom and insight—which knew the difficulties as well as hopes of each gathering He ['Abdu'l-Bahá] addressed.'"[22]

During his travels, Louis, following the example he learned from 'Abdu'l-Bahá, would rise at dawn to offer his prayers.[23] According to Roy Williams, a close friend who accompanied Louis on teaching trips to the South, "'He rose early before sunrise and put on the floor a clean sheet of the daily newspaper or whatever he could obtain as a prayer rug. He would bow down and utter the prayer of praise and glorification. His mind was at peace, his heart was at peace, his conscience was unscathed.'"[24]

Morrison writes, "Like 'Abdu'l-Bahá, he found in the experience of teaching the strength to continue the pace for months at a time."[25] Louis wrote, "'It is really most heartening and inspiring to see the happiness of people when they hear the Glad Tidings of the Kingdom. . . . And the compliments they pay the teacher would be enough to give any one "the big head." . . . So when complimented after an address I often find myself saying to 'Abdu'l-Bahá "This praise is all Thine!"'"[26] Morrison notes, "The satisfaction of finding receptive listeners made the difficulties and hardships of his travels seem insignificant."[27] And she affirms, "In his efforts to eradicate prejudice of all kinds he found encouragement in small victories."[28] Similar to how the Master knew the value of the use of humor, Louis' "sense of humor was another source of strength and balance" for him.[29]

Louis also benefited enormously from the guidance of Shoghi Effendi, who in 1921 succeeded 'Abdu'l-Bahá as the head of the

Bahá'í Faith following His passing. On one occasion, Shoghi Effendi reminded some Bahá'í pilgrims of the high regard in which 'Abdu'l-Bahá held Louis: "'Have the friends read the Master's teachings upon racial amity? Have they enough teaching upon this feature of the Cause? Do they understand its great importance? Do they know of the Master's fearless example in His attitude toward Mr. Gregory in Washington and elsewhere?'"[30]

Louis undoubtedly knew of Shoghi Effendi's sublime descriptions of the Master, including this one: "He is, and should for all time be regarded, first and foremost, as the Center and Pivot of Bahá'u'lláh's peerless and all-enfolding Covenant . . . the perfect Exemplar of His teachings . . . the embodiment of every Bahá'í ideal . . . the Mainspring of the Oneness of Humanity, the Ensign of the Most Great Peace . . . styles and titles that are implicit and find their truest, their highest and fairest expression in the magic name 'Abdu'l-Bahá."[31]

In this connection, Shoghi Effendi also advised, "Let them call to mind, fearlessly and determinedly, the example and conduct of 'Abdu'lBahá while in their midst. Let them remember His courage, His genuine love, His informal and indiscriminating fellowship, His contempt for and impatience of criticism, tempered by His tact and wisdom. Let them revive and perpetuate the memory of those unforgettable and historic episodes and occasions on which He so strikingly demonstrated His keen sense of justice, His spontaneous sympathy for the downtrodden, His ever-abiding sense of the oneness of the human race, His overflowing love for its members, and His displeasure with those who dared to flout His wishes, to deride His methods, to challenge His principles, or to nullify His acts."[32]

'Abdu'l-Bahá did not limit His guidance on race relations to His visit to North America. For example, a Black man from South Africa once visited 'Abdu'l-Bahá in London during His visit there in 1912. He said "that even now no white people really cared very much for the black man."[33] 'Abdu'l-Bahá reportedly replied:

> Compare the present time and the feeling towards the coloured people now, with the state of feeling two or three hundred

> years ago, and see how much better it is at present. In a short time the relationship between the coloured and white people will still further improve, and bye and bye no difference will be felt between them. . . . In the sight of God colour makes no difference at all, He looks at the hearts of men. That which God desires from men is the heart. A black man with a good character is far superior to a white man with a character that is less good.[34]

Even if Louis had not heard of this experience, he likely would have appreciated that ‘Abdu’l-Bahá emphasized that substantial improvements in race relations would be made in the future. He always remembered ‘Abdu’l-Bahá’s spiritually uplifting words to Bahá’ís on the importance of attaining spiritual heights: “For you I desire spiritual distinction . . . you must become . . . distinguished in morals. In the love of God you must become distinguished from all else. You must become distinguished for loving humanity, for unity and accord, for love and justice. In brief, you must become distinguished in all the virtues of the human world—for faithfulness and sincerity, for . . . service to the human world, for love toward every human being, for unity and accord with all people, for removing prejudice and promoting international peace.”[35]

8

SERVING HUMAN ONENESS UNDER THE DIVINE PLAN

In February 1942, a letter was written on behalf of Shoghi Effendi to Sadie Oglesby, a longstanding, active Black Bahá'í. Gayle Morrison writes that in this letter, Shoghi Effendi "detailed the kind of attitude that black Bahá'ís in America required for their own emotional and spiritual well-being and for the ultimate triumph of their vision of unity."[1] Specifically, the Guardian mentioned, "'It is incumbent upon the negro believers to rise above this great test which the attitude of some of their white brethren may present. They must prove their innate equality not by words but by deeds. They must accept the Cause of Bahá'u'lláh for the sake of the Cause, love it, and cling to it, and teach it, and fight for it as their own Cause, forgetful of the shortcomings of others. Any other attitude is unworthy of their faith.'"[2]

The letter also advises: "Proud and happy in the praises which even Bahá'u'lláh Himself has bestowed upon them, they must feel He revealed Himself for them and every other down-trodden race, loves them, and will help them to attain their destiny . . . the negro friends must not waste their precious opportunity to serve the Faith, in these momentous days, by dwelling on the admitted short comings of the white friends. They must arise and serve and teach, confident of the future they are building, a future in which we know these barriers will have once and for all been overcome."[3]

Gayle Morrison herself has observed that "So fully did Louis Gregory exemplify this attitude—so completely, yet mildly, did he disregard conventional barriers—that in a sense, he already existed in that future. He was its best advertisement in a painfully divided age."[4]

Louis was the "touchstone of the principle of oneness in American Bahá'í history."[5] His extraordinary efforts to spread Bahá'u'lláh's teachings on the elimination of all forms of prejudice demonstrated he was for nearly four decades "the mainspring behind the work for Race Amity."[6] While the interests of Bahá'ís for improving race relations ebbed and flowed over the years, Louis was steadfast in promoting it. He facilitated race amity meetings and wrote reports of race amity activities in America. He traveled with different white believers to the South and assisted in conducting banquets in honor of the National Association for the Advancement of Colored People. He also endorsed a remarkable statement on race titled *The Divine Call to Race Amity.*"[7] He put the Bahá'í vision of ideal race relations into practice, and he gradually realized that the evolving influence of "the society-building power" of the Bahá'í teachings, as described by Shoghi Effendi,[8] would eventually enable individuals to dispel the false beliefs regarding white supremacy and Black inferiority. Divisive narratives about racial differences would eventually end.

He spread knowledge of Bahá'í teachings through a diversity of activities, all of which tied together and supported one another, including initiating and maintaining contacts with prominent figures. Under the guidance and direction of 'Abdu'l-Bahá and Shoghi Effendi, he had a sense of focus and urgency. Within the scope of his activities, serving the oneness of humanity came first in his life.

For most of his adult life, Louis was an unpaid volunteer Bahá'í race amity worker. Harland Ober writes, "Living in the utmost simplicity, sacrificing at every turn, he spoke in schools, colleges, churches, forums, conferences and with individuals throughout the land. With a marvelous blending of humility and courage, of tenderness and adamantine firmness and steadfastness, he met high and low, rich and poor, educated and ignorant, and gave to them the cup of the Water of Life [the Bahá'í teachings]."[9]

He faced numerous slights and indignities promoting the removal of prejudice. On a visit, for example, to see a prominent Bahá'í family in New York City, he was forced to take the service elevator, rather than the regular elevator, to their apartment. He refused to let the insult bother him. On another occasion, he was denied accommodation in a Pullman train car. Not feeling well, he had purchased a Pullman ticket in order to rest on a trip to the South. When he refused the order to move to the inferior train section designated for Black passengers, he was arrested and spent a night in a Kentucky jail.[10]

Louis never felt he was doing too much. He taught the Faith to thousands and thousands of people. He outlined a practical approach to being a Bahá'í teacher in a letter to Joseph Hannen. He wrote, "'The Bahá'í teacher must maintain a state of happiness if he is to do his work effectively. And this seems possible only by constant prayer and . . . ceaseless activity. Otherwise the well-authenticated reports of cruel injustices and crimes against defenseless peoples would entirely absorb the powers of concentration.'"[11]

In all his activities, he was convinced that 'Abdu'l-Bahá made his achievements possible through His assurance of assistance and confirmation. Louis' commitment to human oneness was an experience larger than his family, larger than his race, and larger than his country.

In a letter in 1909 to W. E. B. DuBois, Louis encouraged DuBois to continue his study of the Bahá'í teachings. Louis wrote, ". . . . general & specific instructions of the Faith on race relations are summarized by Shoghi Effendi in *The Advent of Divine Justice* which you doubtless have read. . . . [W]hen a person accepts the Faith he must abandon all prejudices. . . . Its [the Bahá'ís Faith's] mysterious Power is indicated by its ability to transform people whose views are diametrically opposed to its ideals and to give them new minds and new hearts. . . ."[12]

The transformative "mysterious Power" for the creation of "new minds and new hearts" he referred to was the influence of the Word of God as revealed in the Bahá'í Revelation. He likely sensed, based on his personal association with DuBois since at least 1912, and his study of some of DuBois' publications, that what Shoghi Effendi wrote in *The Advent of Divine Justice* regarding issues of racial unity would captivate DuBois.[13] There was something both sincerely respectful and kind about his sharing with DuBois in this letter that "'It [Baha'u'llah's Revelation] is here in the South uniting the races as nothing else has ever done or can do. It is creating the bond that is permanent, not the ephemeral bond of the old order. . . .'"[14]

This transformative power of the Bahá'í Faith helped Louis achieve a spiritual transcendence over racial prejudice and enabled him to overcome the difficulties of teaching in the South. And in spite of the challenges of teaching the Faith in this area of the United States, Louis was impressed by signs of change in the South. From his interactions with youth, religious and other leaders, and educators, he realized that substantial improvements were gradually being made. Interracial meetings were being held, and the unspoken rule that the races must not eat together was gradually being broken.[15]

Teaching the Faith had become one of his goals in life, and he was always on the road. During his Southern lecturing tour in 1915, for example, he taught the Faith to many in Memphis and Nashville, Tennessee, and in Tallahassee, Florida. He spoke to almost five thousand people of diverse backgrounds, and further speaking engagements during that trip brought the total of people who had heard him speak to about twenty thousand, many of them students.[16]

Louis was an outstanding public speaker and felt comfortable in both small and large gatherings. In spite of his efforts to convey Bahá'í teachings on love, unity, and justice, attempts were still made to humiliate him. Notwithstanding, his carriage—a symbol of the inner conviction of the inherent nobility of his character—was always straight and upright. Once, white university students in Pittsburgh, having heard of Louis' speaking ability, invited him to give a lecture. However, when he arrived in Pittsburgh, the students sent to meet him at the station had not expected that they would have to provide hospitality for a Black man. They excused themselves and departed, and Louis spent the night in the station's waiting room. The next day, he gave his talk, and he received a standing ovation. The student group apologized for its biased treatment, and Louis was invited to return and speak any time he could.[17]

Bi-Racial Teaching Teams

The services Louis rendered for interracial unity were also under the guidance and directions provided by Shoghi Effendi in the first Seven Year Plan (1937–1944) and the second Seven Year Plan (1946–1953). Over the years, Bahá'í communities around the world have been given national and global plans devised by Shoghi Effendi and the Universal House of Justice. These Plans have provided guidance to Bahá'í institutions and individuals in connection with the implementation of the Divine Plan, which was set in motion by 'Abdu'l-Bahá.

For instance, Shoghi Effendi's letter to American believers of 1938, titled *The Advent of Divine Justice,* indicates that members of the Bahá'í Faith must manifest in all their activities the spiritual prerequisites of rectitude of conduct, a chaste and holy life, and freedom from all forms of prejudice.[18] Filled with extensive excerpts from Bahá'u'lláh's and 'Abdu'l-Bahá's writings, the letter emphasized that Blacks and whites were equally responsible for establishing harmony between their races.[19]

Also in connection with the spread of the Faith, Shoghi Effendi, in another letter, suggested that a teaching team made up of a white and Black Bahá'í should travel together into the southern United States to demonstrate brotherhood in action while spreading Bahá'í teachings.[20] In 1931, Louis was at the forefront of this initiative. He visited the states of Georgia, Alabama, Tennessee, and Ohio with a white Bahá'í, Willard McKay, a former university teacher. McKay wrote, "Louis thinks this is the first time a White man and a Coloured man have traveled together on terms of equality riding on public conveyance though the Southern states."[21]

Louis and Willard ate together, and they shared the same room most of the time. They also sat together in the back of the cheapest buses and trains. Some Blacks and whites were astonished to see them traveling together as equals, but in general, members of both races treated them with courtesy.[22]

At Tuskegee Institute in Tuskegee, Alabama, many Black students and their teachers were familiar with the Bahá'í teachings brought to them on Louis' earlier visits. Willard explained what their biracial service meant for Black students: "'I was equal to them. Eating together was a taboo. It was a revolution against the idea that Black people were to be shut out from the Whites. That's one meaning. When Bahá'u'lláh said Oneness, He meant the end of all taboos. People are equal.'"[23]

Later, Willard's wife, Doris McKay, asked him, "'Was there any bad feelings on the part of the students? You must have experienced some resentment against the White race?'" "'Absolutely none,'" Willard responded. "'There was a desire to be understood and loved by me that sometimes brought tears to my eyes. They couldn't help seeing that I loved them, so they loved me too. It went beyond race.'"[24]

On another occasion, a student asked him: "Why don't white folks like Negroes?" "What can we do to overcome the prejudice against us?" . . . "In your personal opinion is prejudice against Negroes . . . due to jealousy or to the inferiority of the Negro?" "Why do white and colored children play together but tend to separate as they grow older?"[25]

Perhaps that student was looking for an affirmation of his own hopes and dreams; an assurance that racial prejudice wouldn't wound him anymore. Maybe he was wondering why, as said in a letter written on behalf of Shoghi Effendi, "The Negroes, . . . one might say, . . . epitomise the feelings of colour prejudice so rife in the United States."[26] Louis and Willard knew the answer to that student's questions: "Bahá'u'lláh declares that all forms of prejudice must be abandoned . . ."[27]

McKay went on to say, "'I was overwhelmed with love, for what I sensed was the spiritual potency of the Black soul. . . . When our two races unite in this mission to spread the word of Bahá'u'lláh there was a blending of qualities and spiritual chemistry that overcome obstacles. Louis and I prayed sincerely every day. We love humanity. By the grace of God, we prevailed.'"[28]

At Tuskegee, they met with George Washington Carver, the world-famous Black agriculturalist and chemist, who appreciated the Bahá'í teachings that called for interracial unity. In a letter to Roy C. Wilhelm, a white Bahá'í in New York City who had discussed the Bahá'í teachings with him and several other Black intellectuals, Carver wrote, "'I am happy to know that the Christ-like gospel of good will is growing throughout the world. You hold in your organization the key that will settle all our difficulties [of race relations], real and imaginary.'"[29]

Louis said that working with Willard was one of the "'crowning experiences of his life,'" a "'fulfillment of the dreams of equality,'" and "'a testament to the viability of the Bahá'í path to reconstruction, and a compensation for the manifold sacrifices, hardships, and lonely humiliations he had endured along the way. . . .'"[30] Speaking with admiration of Louis' humility, Willard wrote of him: "'He is really a man who would be a great hero to his valet [personal male attendant], if he had one. In his case, the more intimate the association, the greater the love and admiration. . . .'"[31]

Both men were inspired that Shoghi Effendi expressed his "'deepest appreciation of their remarkable and historic services.'" He wrote, "'We all feel indebted to them for their heroic efforts.'"[32]

Another white Bahá'í who traveled in the South with Louis, Charles Wragg, said, "'we sometimes received abrasive reactions. . . . It was on such occasions that his facial expressions were most illuminative, changing quickly from one of anguish to a completely passive inward-look, as though searching his innermost being and beyond for a solution. . . . This was his invariable reaction to difficulties and problems.'" He went on to recall: "'I never saw him show anger, impatience or resentment, always it seemed to be an expression of earnest self-searching and seeking for guidance from beyond self-identity. I imagine that this was a reason why 'Abdu'l-Bahá said of him: "He is pure gold."'"[33]

Shoghi Effendi, in a letter to Mr. Wragg written on his behalf, commended Mr. Wragg for his service during his travels with Louis: "He trusts that this example you have set will be followed by many Bahá'ís + before long we will see mixed groups of White + coloured Bahá'ís traveling together + associating with one another very closely."[34]

The Tablets of the Divine Plan

Coming back to Louis' services under 'Abdu'l-Baha's ministry, during World War I, 'Abdu'l-Bahá addressed a series of letters to the Bahá'ís in North America, The Tablets of the Divine Plan, for the worldwide propagation of Bahá'u'lláh's message of world unity. Some were published in 1916. Two of the Tablets called for Bahá'ís in the Southern States to establish the Faith more extensively in the region.[35]

Inspired by these Tablets, Louis visited fourteen of the sixteen southern states. He spoke to high and low alike at colleges, churches, and social meetings. Another phase of the Divine Plan was launched in 1919. Once again, he accepted 'Abdu'l-Bahá's calls for sacrificial efforts to achieve the Plan's goals "without hesitation, as he always had, and proceeded to obey them, as if they were a personal instruction. . . ."[36] In response to these calls, Louis once embarked on a nearly three-year period of uninterrupted travel in the South.[37]

In 1916, Roy Williams, a young, newly declared Black Bahá'í whom Louis had mentored in Washington, DC, often traveled with him in the South. In 1919–1921, he accompanied Louis many times as he crisscrossed the Southern region. Roy once told Louis, "'We'll try to change the attitude of the people . . .'" After some experience, Roy further observed, "'We were tackling a problem that was too deep for one man or two men. We had the cooperation of others. . . . This journey seemed rather hapless and haphazard to us but as we picked up the trail to our astonishment we . . . kept out of harm's way and out of trouble with the people . . . I do not know now how we managed to do these things. I do not know how we managed to survive.'"[38] Janet Ruhe-Schoen writes, "[T]hey often went with just two meals a day and gave their rousing talks on empty stomachs."[39]

Every Southern city had its own peculiar Jim Crow laws, customs, social taboos, and expectations. For instance, some places strictly required that Black persons step off sidewalks while passing white persons and keep their heads, eyes, and shoulders bent down in public. Sometimes Louis and Roy found no comfortable place to sleep or eat because their skin color barred them from public accommodations. Sometimes they even slept in police stations. When needed, Louis reached out to people he knew from college or from professional associations who might provide assistance in obtaining accommodations and in holding meetings.[40]

Whenever he spoke from podiums and pulpits, he made certain that no one felt he had come to town for financial gain. He wouldn't accept any amount of financial contributions for his visits. He didn't charge a lecture fee or let anyone take up a collection on his behalf, and he observed that a friend of his would have thought he had gone insane if he ever found out that he never accepted a fee or contribution for his presentations.[41]

During these times, it was often impossible to get an interracial group together. Some Black people were anxious to hear what he had to say, but fear held them back from attending his talks. In some cities, such as Houston, Texas, he had to be interviewed by the police department before he could speak to anyone.[42]

Beyond this social context, the challenge some Bahá'ís faced for achieving the Plan's goals set by 'Abdu'l-Bahá was compounded when, in November 1921, He passed away. Some American believers had difficulty transferring their personal loyalty to Shoghi Effendi, whom 'Abdu'l-Bahá had appointed as His successor, along with the Universal House of Justice. Louis, however, had no difficulty accepting Shoghi Effendi's position as head of the Faith. Absolutely confident in the new period the Faith had entered, he continued the work 'Abdu'l-Bahá had given him. During his teaching trips, he helped maintain unity, confidence, and optimism within Bahá'í communities. As Gayle Morrison has noted, "In America the ability of the Bahá'ís to transfer the focus of their highly personal loyalty from 'Abdu'l-Bahá to Shoghi Effendi was tested by a number of agitators. Under the circumstances, the energies of the active Bahá'ís were spent on maintaining unity and optimism more than on expansion. Louis Gregory was among the few who addressed both needs. He continued to travel extensively, teaching the Faith to new people as always and providing invaluable encouragement to the Bahá'ís themselves."[43]

Coast to Coast Lecture Teaching

Louis' contributions were particularly decisive during his long travel-teaching journey that took place in 1920 and 1921. He crisscrossed the United States from coast to coast and reached several thousands with the Bahá'í message.[44]

He visited Chicago once again. He had been there with 'Abdu'l-Bahá in 1912 when the Master had given a talk at the Fourth Annual Conference of the NAACP. In His address, 'Abdu'l-Bahá had explained how man has been made in the image of God: "This standard can be no other than the divine virtues which are revealed in him. . . . The character and purity of the heart is of all importance. . . . inasmuch as God has endowed man with such favor that he is called the image of God, this is truly a supreme perfection of attainment, a divine station which is not to be sacrificed by the mere accident of color."[45]

During his 1921 visit to Chicago, the National Teaching Committee noted that he had "'[a]n average of a meeting a day, sometimes more . . . [and] [h]undreds were given the Message.'"[46]

In Minnesota, a Bahá'í said Louis' visit made Bahá'ís more united and caused an unprecedented public interest in the Faith. From Duluth, Louis reported that the "'Bahá'í Teachings have now reached practically all the colored and many thousands of white people.'"[47]

In Denver, he spoke at twenty-two meetings and reached "all classes" in a variety of churches and organizations. He gave a talk to eight hundred students at the Central High School in Pueblo, Colorado. He remarked in his report to the National Teaching Committee, "'You know that youngsters are not inclined to restraint when happy. I have never seen nothing like the ovation they accorded since visiting Tuskegee Institute some years ago. The Superintendent of Schools, Principal [and] fifty-two teachers, joined in the enthusiasm, and extended a cordial invitation to return.'"[48]

He had full speaking schedules also in Salt Lake City, Utah; Butte and Helena, Montana; and Spokane and Seattle, Washington.[49] "'Words cannot express what Mr. Gregory's visit in Seattle has meant—not only to the Bahá'ís but to the whole community,'" the Local Spiritual Assembly of Seattle wrote in gratitude. "'The spirit of unity and harmony manifested was unusual. Our dear brother is such a wonderfully illumined soul; we just kept him going at "top-notch speed," sending out his bright rays to at least two audiences a day and sometimes as many as four. . . . He was always so willing and gracious about everything. . . .'"[50]

Finally, Louis also visited Topeka, Kansas; Kansas City and St. Louis, Missouri; Springfield and Urbana, Illinois; Portland, Oregon; Phoenix, Arizona; Tulsa and Oklahoma City, Oklahoma; and Berkeley and Los Angeles, California.[51] A member of the Local Spiritual Assembly of Portland noted that Louis called on sick Bahá'ís and those who could not get out to hear his talks.[52]

The National Teaching Committee, composed of Bahá'ís appointed by the National Spiritual Assembly to spread teachings of the Faith throughout the country, commended Louis' coast to coast journey as "'one of the most brilliant Bahá'í Teaching Tours we have ever been privileged to have in this country.'"[53]

Gayle Morrison notes the following: "Louis Gregory's activities during the early years of the Guardianship were in themselves a sign of life in the American Bahá'í community. At the annual convention in 1922, the first after the loss of 'Abdu'l-Bahá, the National Teaching Committee described Mr. Gregory's travels during the previous months not only as one of the highlights of the year but as a milestone in the history of the Bahá'í Faith in America."[54] The Committee's secretary, Mariam Haney, also told the delegates at the annual convention: "'Every one, I think, appreciates to the fullest extent the work accomplished in this country from coast to coast the last year by Mr. Gregory.'"[55]

Mariam Haney continued, "'I do not think we have had anything that approached it in any way in the 24 years or since 1895 when the Cause first started in this country. Now there are many reasons why I think this was a very extraordinary work from a spiritual standpoint, because it is the first time that any teacher so marvelously illumined as Mr. Gregory has been able to reach thousand[s] and thousands of people, colored and white. This is why we consider it a very remarkable spiritual work. . . . 'Abdu'l-Bahá said more than once that he [Mr. Gregory] would be the cause of the guidance of both races. He was received warmly in every direction, and had very wonderful opportunities for service through the doors that were opened to him.'"[56]

As noted by Gayle Morrison, ". . . although he [Louis Gregory] had been strongly attached to 'Abdu'l-Bahá, he had no difficulty in accepting the authority of Shoghi Effendi, no trepidation about the future progress of the Cause, and no doubt about the importance of continuing the work that 'Abdu'l-Bahá had given him. The latter point was cited by the National Teaching Committee as having been 'first and foremost' in Mr. Gregory's success. The second element pointed out by the committee was his whole-hearted devotion and 'absolute attention' to 'Abdu'l-Bahá, and the third was Mr. Gregory's humility as a teacher."[57]

According to Gayle Morrison, "Louis Gregory's success was in part a reflection of his fundamental confidence in the new period that the Bahá'í Faith had entered. His attitude toward the Guardian revealed from the beginning the quality that Bahá'ís term firmness in the Covenant of Baha'u'llah, a loyalty to the central figures and institutions of the Faith so unshakeable that it prevents disunity and eventual schism."[58]

In her brilliant article, "A New Creation: The Power of the Covenant in the Life of Louis Gregory," Gayle Morrison shows that in each of his fields of service, Louis was guided and energized by "firmness in the Covenant," a quality which emphasizes steadfastly following Bahá'í teachings. His manifestation of this quality was related "to his dynamic relationship with 'Abdu'l-Bahá and Shoghi Effendi as focal points of covenantal authority."[59] Morrison further writes, "'O thou who art firm in the Covenant!' were the words with which 'Abdu'l-Bahá began four of nine letters that He addressed to Louis Gregory." She further notes: "it [the salutation] appears in perhaps three to five percent of 'Abdu'l-Bahá's published letters (tablets) addressed to His followers in the West. Most of the recipients are recognized today as having been among the outstanding, active dedicated early Bahá'ís. Yet the salutation 'O thou who art firm in the Covenant!' was never more aptly applied than to Gregory."[60]

Horace Holley, secretary of the National Spiritual Assembly of the United States, wrote to Louis, "'The conditions of danger and sacrifice under which you are teaching seems to me to approximate more closely the early days of the Revelation in Persia than can be found anywhere else in the West at this time. God bless you!'"[61]

Gayle Morrison has written: "His voice reaches across barriers of race and class, even of time and distance, to form lasting bonds of affinity. Thirty years after his passing, he is still a living presence, signaling hope for a changing world."[62] In her published essay *Above All Barriers,* about Louis' life and services, Elsie Austin notes:

> The quality and beauty of the life of a godly man survive both time and death, because they have been multiplied in the lives of others. We know a man is good by the way he finds and inspires goodness in the lives of others . . . This is the kind of goodness and greatness which crosses the oceans, climbs the mountains, bridges the great distances, and goes through the subtle barriers—because it passes from heart to heart. Louis Gregory had this goodness and greatness. 'Abdu'l-Bahá said of him: "He is like pure gold. That is why he is acceptable in any market, and is current in every country." The noble character and distinguished service of this much loved man made him achieve one of the highest spiritual stations in the Bahá'í Faith.

> The memory of his human personality is treasured by those who saw and will never forget that radiant countenance, the dignity, the genuine courtesy, the kindness, the gentle humor, the sweetness of speech, and the spiritual dedication which illumined his person. The effects of his saintly life will bear endless fruit in the changed hearts, the uplifted spirits, the renewed courage, and the dedicated service he brought and is to bring in the lives which come under his influence. Louis Gregory's story is an illustration of God's guidance to a receptive soul.[63]

Race Amity Conventions

Another groundbreaking activity in which Louis was a key participant was the first Race Amity Convention, which was held in Washington, DC in 1921. Other conventions were soon held in several other American cities, and over time, Louis became heavily involved in speaking at and organizing some of these conventions, which made an unequivocal public statement on the Bahá'í approach to addressing racial prejudice and the oneness of humanity.[64]

The first National Race Amity Convention was held in Washington, DC on May 19–21, 1921.[65] The initiative was quite radical for that time, as it was the first large interracial gathering in the capital city since the "Red Summer" (during 1919) of racial riots in America. The race riots in Washington, DC, of 1919, and in other cities, must have strengthened Louis' resolve to improve race relations, and during this time, he visited several riot-torn cities.

In his report to the National Teaching Committee in 1922, Louis noted, for example, that in Tulsa, which had been "'shaken by a terrible riot in which there was a great loss of life on both sides, and nearly the entire "colored section" was destroyed by incendiary fires . . . "nearly all" of his talks—in churches, public schools, to various organizations, and even to prisoners at the city jail—were given before integrated audiences.'" He continued, "'I am as safe here as anywhere else in creation, for, after all, the only Safety is the Power of the Covenant, which is unlimited.'"[66] During Louis' visit to Helena, Arkansas, shortly after a race riot occurred there in 1919, he gave six public talks on the Bahá'í Faith among "'people who have been in a state of grim pessimism and despair.'"[67]

In 1920, 'Abdu'l-Bahá asked Mrs. Agnes S. Parsons, a white, wealthy, socially prominent Washington, DC Bahá'í, while she was on pilgrimage, to arrange a convention in Washington, DC, for racial amity between the Blacks and whites. In Louis' view, 'Abdu'l-Bahá had made a perfect choice in assigning Agnes Parsons, "'a white Bahá'í of wealth and social prominence,'" to arrange the first amity conference. Louis felt "'[n]o one could question the motives of such a soul, when you consider both her spiritual illumination, devotion etc., added to her worldly station.'"[68]

'Abdu'l-Bahá reportedly described the significance of the Race Amity Convention in this way: "'"Say to this convention that never since the beginning of time has one more important been held. This convention stands for the oneness of humanity; it will become the cause of the enlightenment of America. . . ."'"[69]

Louis loved the audacious plan set in motion by 'Abdu'l-Bahá for promoting unity and concord. He felt it would address "'friction between the races'"[70] and the "'causes of the recent outbreaks [race riots] of race prejudice.'"[71] Louis once wrote: "'The whole matter of racial adjustment [relations] is very difficult and requires a world of patience and effort. . . . without any attitude of superiority on the part of either [Blacks or whites].'"[72]

For advice on arranging the convention, Mrs. Parsons turned to Senator Moses Clapp and other experienced individuals, who gave valuable input. Clapp's suggestions in particular influenced the tenor of the convention. He said that it should strike a positive note toward "'"the spiritual realm."'"[73] When she turned to Louis for advice, he recalled that many people of both races were striving for harmony and understanding. He suggested that it should endeavor to "'be aflame with the Fire of the Divine Love, [so that] the hearts will be powerfully influenced and the effect will be great in all the years to come.'"[74]

Louis' "highest hopes" for the gathering were realized.[75] Two thousand people showed up on the night of May 19th, and each subsequent session over a period of three days drew up to 1,500 people.[76] Many thousands were reached by 19,000 printed invitations circulated in churches, schools, hotels, stores, and other public places, and Louis' active participation in implementing the conference's program inspired others.[77] The conference presented the Bahá'í position that human oneness was the foundation of world peace, global justice, and integration. The aim of the conference went beyond promoting unity between the Black and white race. Instead, the conference embraced the oneness of all ethnicities, nations, and religions.[78]

Louis described the convention as "'the first convention for amity between the white and colored races in America and so far as we know, the world.'"[79] In his speech at the convention, he remarked, "'The divine springtime has appeared and the great enlightened principles, which are the light and progress of the whole world of humanity, are set in motion. These relate . . . to the great law that humanity is one. . . .'"[80]

In his presentation, he observed, "'women . . . must no longer be confined to a limited life but be everywhere recognized as the equal and helpmeet of man.'"[81] For him, the civil rights aspirations of women and of Blacks were not in competition with one another, as some people perceived them to be. Among Louis' most impressive literary achievements over three decades was his published article, titled "Racial Amity in America: An Historical Review," which considered features of the first national convention, as well as local conventions held, for example, in New York, Philadelphia, Chicago, Montreal, Detroit, Pittsburgh, and several other cities.[82]

In summarizing the historic nature of the Washington, DC Race Amity Convention, Morrison notes that it broadened the discourse on interracial accord "beyond the confines of the liberal reform movement" and also introduced "large numbers of people, both black and white"[83] to Bahá'í teachings regarding human oneness. Morrison has also noted the importance of the convention's intangible results: "'Abdu'l-Baha always emphasized the importance of intangible results within the realm of ideas and of social change made meaningful by a change of heart and a new spirit."[84] 'Abdu'l-Bahá was very pleased with the contributions of Mrs. Parsons at his direct request and assured her of "'eternal glory'" and that the Convention "'is conducive to the comfort and ease of the continent of America.'"[85] He wrote to Mrs. Parson with this commendation: "'The Convention, comprising the white and the colored, which thou hadst organized, was like the Mother, from which in near future many other meetings shall be born. But thou wert the founder of this Convention. The importance of every principle is at the beginning, and the first person to raise the banner of the unity of the white and the colored, wert thou. It is certain that it shall bear great results.'"[86]

Louis with Sadie Oglesby and Grace Ober in Montreal, 1927.
(US Bahá'í National Archives)

Under Shoghi Effendi's global leadership of the Bahá'í Faith (1921–1957), Louis continued to constantly share the Faith's teachings on interracial unity with leaders of thought and with the general public. In 1937, for instance, he and Loulie Mathews, chairman and secretary of the amity committee, hosted an interracial banquet in New York. It honored the NAACP and the National Urban League for their promotions of interracial unity. Among the guests were W. E. B. DuBois, who wrote to Ms. Mathews a few days later that "'everyone present was under deep obligations for your (Bahá'í) thoughts and ideals.'"[87] Walter White, secretary of the NAACP, lauded "'the Bahá'í movement as one of the great forces of human understanding.'"[88] A lengthy article in the March 5 edition of the *Chicago Defender* newspaper congratulated the Bahá'í Faith for hosting the banquet, which highlighted the need for "'peace and amity and love of mankind.'"[89]

By this time, the Bahá'í community had come to be recognized by certain influential Black leaders as a credible promoter of interracial cooperation and anti-prejudice in America's race relations.[90] In many ways, Louis laid the groundwork for this development, but he knew more must be accomplished. In 1937, when the Seven Year Plan was devised by Shoghi Effendi,[91] the Gregorys traveled to Haiti to spread Bahá'í teachings. They were happy they could serve together as international volunteer workers for unity after twenty-four years of marriage. Because of governmental opposition to their teaching activities, they stayed only three months, but even in this short period, they were able to discuss the Bahá'í teachings with many interested persons.[92]

Also in his later years, Louis encouraged Blacks and whites to advance oneness. In 1950, for instance, he wrote to J. Waties Waring—a white Federal District Judge in Charleston, South Carolina—and his wife Elizabeth. The judge had decided in a court case that Black and white teachers' salaries should be equal and that certain voting practices were unconstitutional. This couple was intensely disliked by many whites because it was also reported that they entertained Black guests in their home and because Mrs. Waring had spoken to a mixed gathering at the city's Black Y.W.C.A. The judge and his family suffered ostracism by whites who wouldn't speak to them.[93]

In response to Louis' two letters of encouragement in which he enclosed Bahá'í booklets, Judge Waring wrote: "We are indeed happy since we feel sure that we are on the right road, and communications like yours convince us that that is true. . . . It is very heartening to receive letters from decent thinking people like yourself, and Mrs. Waring and I appreciate your kind words about us."[94] At Louis' suggestion, the National Spiritual Assembly wrote the judge an encouraging letter.[95] Two years later, the couple left the city.

9

A MAN FOR SERVING ONENESS

Basking in his choice to serve human and racial oneness, Louis poured his heart and soul into becoming a man, in a way that was completely different from the definition of "manhood," both in his time and in our own time. For the Bahá'í writings say, "That one indeed is a man who, today, dedicateth himself to the service of the entire human race. . . . Blessed and happy is he that ariseth to promote the best interests of the peoples and kindreds of the earth. . . ."[1] It is well known, of course, that the designation *man,* or personhood, applies equally to women. In this connection, 'Abdu'l-Bahá revealed, "The lovers of mankind, these are the superior men, of whatever nation, creed, or color they may be."[2] 'Abdu'l-Bahá also clarified that "'Man is not to be pronounced man simply because of bodily attributes. Man is to be judged according to his intelligence and to his spirit.'"[3]

Feelings of inferiority and doubts about the very meaning of manhood had been ingrained into Black communities as a consequence of slavery. But by a combination of factors, Louis proved he was so spiritually empowered by Bahá'u'lláh's Revelation that he could overcome his own background and America's perverse racial history.

He rose above these humiliating circumstances by being guided by the spiritual values of nobility, by being devoted to the principles of fairness and decency, and by being emboldened to undertake service for the betterment of humanity. He transcended a prejudiced, disunited world in which his manhood was mocked. Serving oneness shaped his sense of self.

Instead of falling victim to the degrading influence of racism, Louis showed children, youth, and men and women of all colors, races, classes, and creeds what they could become, if they wished. Everything Louis grew up experiencing affected the direction of his life of service to humanity. 'Abdu'l-Bahá asked: "[I]s there any deed in the world that would be nobler than service to the common good? Is there any greater blessing conceivable for a man, than that he should become the cause of the education, the development, the prosperity and honor of his fellow-creatures? . . . The highest righteousness of all is for blessed souls . . . to arise and energetically devote themselves to the service of the masses, forgetting their own worldly advantage and working only to serve the general good."[4]

Louis' firmness in the Covenant shielded him from being an unprotected, debilitated victim of the forces of racial prejudice. Morrison reports that he "faced numerous slights and indignities in carrying out his work, but he did not allow himself to be wounded by them."[5] He called on many in his travels throughout the United States to accept the challenge of establishing racial harmony. He was confident of his cause, of its lines of action, and of the abilities of people to engage in meaningful and successful action.

He had learned for his well-being, and for the betterment of the world and its peoples, that he must follow the guidance of 'Abdu'l-Bahá, Who said, "manifest complete love and affection toward all mankind. Do not exalt yourselves above others, but consider all as your equals, recognizing them as the servants of one God . . . be filled with love for every race, and be kind toward the people of all nationalities. Never speak disparagingly of others, but praise without distinction. Pollute not your tongues by speaking evil of another. . . .

[C]onsider your enemies as your friends. . . . Act in such a way that your heart may be free from hatred."[6]

Louis never got the "big head," or vanity, as he called it, and he never exalted himself above anyone. He had learned long ago from his grandmother the importance of freeing his heart from racial hatred. But more than that, he had learned from the Bahá'í teachings that prejudice "is rooted in the heart and can only be annihilated by a transformation of the heart."[7] In a letter to Agnes Parsons, Louis wrote that "'Nothing short of a change of hearts will do'"[8] to become free from all forms of prejudice. He had opened his heart one stormy night long ago on his way to his first Bahá'í meeting so that his own heart might be transformed, so that he could transcend all forms of prejudice, and so that he might do a "'work . . . that would bless humanity.'"[9] And he did so to such an extent that Gayle Morrison remarked: "Louis Gregory lived his life in the forefront of a struggle that is still being waged. The immediacy of his example has the power to inform and to inspire . . . His voice reaches across barriers of race and class, even of time and distance, to form lasting bonds of affinity . . . he is still a living presence, signaling hope for a changing world.[10] He was a humble man constantly striving to strengthen himself spiritually. As Bahá'u'lláh wrote, "This is a matchless Day. Matchless must, likewise, be the tongue that celebrateth the praise of the Desire of all nations, and matchless the deed that aspireth to be acceptable in His sight. The whole human race hath longed for this Day, that perchance it may fulfill that which well beseemeth its station, and is worthy of its destiny. Blessed is the man whom the affairs of the world have failed to deter from recognizing Him Who is the Lord of all things."[11]

In connection with the theme of service which dominated Louis' life, 'Abdu'l-Bahá reminded members of the Bahá'í Faith in America: "Verily, God has chosen you for His love and knowledge; God has chosen you for the worthy service of unifying mankind; God has chosen you for the purpose of investigating reality and promulgating international peace; God has chosen you for the progress and development of humanity, for spreading and proclaiming true education, for the expression of love toward your fellow creatures and the removal of prejudice; God has chosen you to blend together human hearts and give light to the human world. The doors of His generosity are wide, wide open to us; but we must be attentive, alert and mindful, occupied with service to all mankind, appreciating the bestowals of God and ever conforming to His will."[12]

Louis with others in California, 1926. (US Bahá'í National Archives)

Here are some words Louis spoke in 1926 during the National Bahá'í Convention in San Francisco: "'So, among all the different races and groups and classes of people in the world, the ideal of today is co-operation, mutuality, service. If one wants to distinguish himself let him become distinguished as a servant of humanity. Let him stand upon the exalted principle of the oneness of . . . the entire human race. Who-ever stands upon this exalted principle will never be shaken by the shifting sands of time; who-ever stands upon this exalted principle, . . . will move the world.'"[13] And this is what he did!

His extraordinary labors show that he understood, as stated in the Bahá'í writings: "Mere knowledge of principles is not sufficient. We all know and admit that justice is good, but there is need of volition and action to carry out and manifest it . . . Action is essential."[14] He felt he had to help others from all strata of society to, as Shoghi Effendi wrote, "cleanse their souls from every lingering trace of racial animosity."[15] He accepted the challenge with devotion and valor. This is a major part of his legacy.

The following tributes paid to Louis by 'Abdu'l-Bahá, Shoghi Effendi, and the Universal House of Justice indicate the station he achieved.

'Abdu'l-Bahá

O thou who hast an illumined heart! Thou art even as the pupil of the eye, the very wellspring of the light, for God's love hath cast its rays upon thine inmost being and thou hast turned thy face toward the Kingdom of thy Lord.[16]

Do thou consider what a bounty God hath bestowed upon thee in giving thee a husband such as Mr. Gregory who is the essence of the love of God and is a symbol of guidance! How luminous is the face of this person! His character is (like unto) a rose garden.[17]

That pure soul has a heart like unto transparent water. He is like unto pure gold. That is why he is acceptable in any market and is current in every country.[18]

O Thou Wooer of Truth! Thy letter was received. Its contents indicated thy attainment to the Most Great Guidance. Thank God that thou hast attained to such a bounty, discovered the Path of the Kingdom and received the Glad-Tidings of the Universe of the Most High. This Divine Bestowal is conducive to the Everlasting Glory in both worlds. I hope that thou mayest become the Herald of the Kingdom, become the means whereby the white and colored peoples shall close their eyes to racial differences and behold the reality of humanity, and that is the universal unity which is the oneness of the kingdom of the human race, the basic harmony of the world and the appearance of the Bounty of the Almighty. . . .[19]

Shoghi Effendi

You have attained spiritual heights that few indeed can claim to have scaled. You have displayed a spirit that few, if any, can equal.[20]

Dear and precious co-worker: The spirit which you have demonstrated . . . is indeed worthy of the praise and admiration of the Supreme Concourse. The place you occupy in my heart and the measure of admiration I cherish for the sublimity of your faith, I cannot describe. . . . My prayers will accompany you, wherever you may be. With a heart filled with love and gratitude, Your true brother. . . .[21]

My self-sacrificing brother in ʻAbdu'l-Bahá! Your splendid activities, your single-mindedness and devotion to the great work you are doing for the Cause is an inspiration to me in my task and a refreshment in the midst of my arduous duties. He who loved you, admired your capacity and was confident in your success is surely guiding every step you take and addresses you from on high, "Well done, (Marhaba, Marhaba) my good and faithful friend!" What greater reward than the satisfaction and the good-pleasure of our dear Master which I am certain you have fully earned? I read the account of your travels with heartfelt joy and gratitude and I will continue to pray for you that you may be enabled to achieve still greater things for so glorious and mighty a Cause.[22]

My very dear & precious coworker: Your letter has infused strength and joy in my heart. . . . I have nothing but admiration and gratitude for the heroic constancy, mature wisdom, tireless energy, and shining love with which you are conducting your ever-expanding work of service to the Cause of Bahá'u'lláh. You hardly realize what a help you are to me in my arduous work. Your grateful brother. . . .[23]

The Universal House of Justice

You also may wish to read about the life of the Hand of the Cause of God Louis Gregory to see how 'Abdu'l-Bahá's unbounded love so transformed him that he in turn became a potent instrument in effecting transformation in others, enabling him to triumph over racial prejudice at one of the saddest and worst periods of racial discrimination in the history of the United States. Look with the eye of fairness at how much things have changed for the better since that time, and be confident that the example Mr. Gregory set, if followed, can effect greater changes than have already occurred.[24]

In this respect, the powerful example of the Hand of the Cause Louis Gregory is an invaluable source of inspiration and encouragement.[25]

10 / PASSING

Mr. Gregory passed on July 30, 1951. Shoghi Effendi sent the following cable: "PROFOUNDLY DEPLORE GRIEVOUS LOSS OF DEARLY BELOVED, NOBLE-MINDED, GOLDEN-HEARTED LOUIS GREGORY, PRIDE AND EXAMPLE TO THE NEGRO ADHERENTS OF THE FAITH. KEENLY FEEL LOSS OF ONE SO LOVED, ADMIRED AND TRUSTED BY 'ABDU'L-BAHÁ. DESERVES RANK OF FIRST HAND OF THE CAUSE OF HIS RACE. RISING BAHÁ'Í GENERATION IN AFRICAN CONTINENT WILL GLORY IN HIS MEMORY AND EMULATE HIS EXAMPLE. ADVISE HOLD MEMORIAL GATHERING IN TEMPLE IN TOKEN RECOGNITION OF HIS UNIQUE POSITION, OUTSTANDING SERVICES."[1]

In the memorial service for Hand of the Cause of God Louis George Gregory, called for by Shoghi Effendi and held at the Bahá'í House of Worship in Wilmette, Illinois, Mrs. Louise Mathew Gregory read a prayer for the progress of the soul of her departed husband.[2] For forty years, they had been united in love for their Faith, love for each other, and love for all people.

On May 20, 1956, Mrs. Louise Mathew Gregory passed away at the age of ninety-six. The cable from Shoghi Effendi to the National Spiritual Assembly of the Bahá'ís of America read: "GRIEVED BY NEWS OF PASSING OF FAITHFUL, CONSECRATED HANDMAID OF 'ABDU'L-BAHÁ. CONFIDENT OF RICH REWARD IN THE KINGDOM. HER PIONEER SERVICES HIGHLY MERITORIOUS."[3]

Gayle Morrison observed that while Shoghi Effendi's cablegram of Mr. Gregory's passing linked him with Africa: "Shoghi Effendi was not categorizing Louis Gregory by race or relegating him to a position of importance only in the Pan-African sphere. Since the time of 'Abdu'l-Bahá, the Bahá'í teachings had always linked racial unity in America to the cause of world peace. . . . [T]he Guardian felt strongly that the development of the Faith among blacks in America was part of a general spiritual 'upsurge' of the nonwhite peoples of the world prerequisite to the establishment of world order. . . . Thus Louis Gregory's effort to unite the races—the task given to him by 'Abdu'l-Bahá—was lifted to the global level, and his lifetime of service was given international significance on his passing."[4]

Mr. Gregory chose—from his childhood growing up as the son of former slaves to his last breath as a Bahá'í teacher—to direct his life toward proclaiming the oneness of humanity and teaching the Bahá'í Faith. His discovery of Bahá'u'lláh as the latest Manifestation of God, and His message of humanity as one family, freed his soul from all racial oppression. He embodied, in every way possible, the phrase "lover of humanity." He was Louis George Gregory, Hand of the Cause of God.

Louis George Gregory, Hand of the Cause of God.
(US Bahá'í National Archives)

NOTES

Acknowledgments

1. Louis Venters, *No Jim Crow Church: The Origins of South Carolina's Bahá'í Community,* p. 5.
2. Richard Thomas, in Gwendolyn Etter-Lewis and Richard Thomas, *Lights of the Spirit: Historical Portraits of Black Bahá'ís in North America 1898–2000,* p. 26.
3. Gayle Morrison, *To Move the World,* p. xviii.

Introduction

1. Gayle Morrison, *To Move the World,* p. 29.
2. Shoghi Effendi, *The World Order of Bahá'u'lláh,* p. 42.
3. Gayle Morrison, *To Move the World,* p. 29.
4. Louis Gregory, quoted in Gayle Morrison, *To Move the World,* pp. 28–29.
5. Glenford Mitchell, quoted in Gayle Morrison, *To Move the World,* p. xi.
6. 'Abdu'l-Bahá, quoted in Gayle Morrison, *To Move the World,* pp. xvi and xviii.
7. Gayle Morrison, *To Move the World,* p. 61.
8. Louis Gregory, quoted in Gayle Morrison, *To Move the World,* p. 61.
9. Janet Ruhe-Schoen, *Champions of Oneness: Louis Gregory and His Shining Circle,* p. 70.

10. Gayle Morrison, *To Move the World,* p. 28.
11. Ibid., p. xx.
12. Glenford Mitchell, quoted in ibid., p. xviii.
13. Gayle Morrison, *To Move the World,* p. xxiii.
14. Ibid., p. 316.
15. May Maxwell, quoted in Gayle Morrison, *To Move the World,* p. 316.
16. Lyrics of Negro Spiritual "I'm So Glad Trouble Don't Last Always," https://www.negrospirituals.com/songs/i_m_so_glad_trouble_don_t_last_always.htm.
17. Louis Gregory, quoted in Gayle Morrison, *To Move the World,* p. 321.
18. 'Abdu'l-Bahá, *'Abdu'l-Bahá in London,* p. 28.
19. Shoghi Effendi, *Bahá'í Administration,* p. 129.
20. Shoghi Effendi, *The Advent of Divine Justice,* ¶58.
21. Ibid., ¶63.
22. Louis Gregory, quoted in Gayle Morrison, *To Move the World,* p. 321.
23. Bahá'u'lláh, *Tablets of Bahá'u'lláh,* p. 129.
24. 'Abdu'l-Bahá, *The Secret of Divine Civilization,* no. 173.
25. 'Abdu'l-Bahá, *Selections from the Writings of 'Abdu'l-Bahá,* nos. 15.7.
26. Shoghi Effendi, quoted in Gayle Morrison, *To Move the World,* p. 294.
27. Shoghi Effendi, quoted in Ruḥiyyih Khánum, *The Guardian of the Bahá'í Faith,* p. 192.
28. Shoghi Effendi, *The Advent of Divine Justice,* ¶54.
29. Louis Gregory, "Light on Basic Unity," *The Bahá'í World,* vol. 4 (1930–1932): 487.
30. Louis Gregory, quoted in Janet Ruhe-Schoen, *Champions of Oneness: Louis Gregory and His Shining Circle,* p. 204.
31. Louis Gregory, quoted in Gayle Morrison, *To Move the World,* p. 312.
32. 'Abdu'l-Bahá, *The Promulgation of Universal Peace,* pp. 348–49.

33. In His Will and Testament, 'Abdu'l-Bahá indicated the obligations of the Hands of the Cause of God: "The obligations of the Hands of the Cause of God are to diffuse the Divine Fragrances, to edify the souls of men, to promote learning, to improve the character of all men and to be, at all times and under all conditions, sanctified and detached from earthly things. They must manifest the fear of God by their conduct, their manners, their deeds and their words" ('Abdu'l-Bahá, *The Will and Testament of 'Abdu'l-Bahá*, p. 13).
34. Shoghi Effendi, quoted in Gayle Morrison, *To Move the World*, p. 317.
35. 'Abdu'l-Bahá, quoted in Shoghi Effendi, *The Advent of Divine Justice*, ¶56.
36. Ibid.
37. Ibid.
38. Ibid.
39. James Cobb, quoted in Gayle Morrison, *To Move the World*, p. 18.

1 / Starting from Home: A Good Beginning

1. Gayle Morrison, *To Move the World*, p. 35.
2. 'Abdu'l-Bahá, quoted in ibid., p. 7.
3. Louis Venters, *No Jim Crow Church: The Origins of South Carolina's Bahá'í Community*, p. 47.
4. Louis Gregory, quoted in ibid., p. 35.
5. W. E. B. DuBois, "Black Reconstruction, an Essay Toward a History of the Part Which Black Folk Played in the Attempt to Reconstruct Democracy in America, 1860–1880."
6. Louis Gregory, "A Gift of Race Enlightenment," *World Order*, Volume 2, p. 39, https://bahai.works/World_Order/Volume_2/Issue_1/Text#pg36.
7. Roy Williams, quoted in Janet Ruhe-Schoen, *Champions of Oneness: Louis Gregory and His Shining Circle*, p. 30.
8. Gayle Morrison, *To Move the World*, p. 4.
9. Ibid., p. 103.

10. Venters, *No Jim Crow Church: The Origins of South Carolina's Bahá'í Community,* p. 83.
11. Ibid., 49–50.
12. Gayle Morrison, *To Move the World,* pp. 46-47.
13. Janet Ruhe-Schoen, *Champions of Oneness: Louis Gregory and His Shining Circle,* p. 86.
14. Louis Gregory, "Racial Amity in America: An Historical Review," *The Bahá'í World,* vol. 7 (1936–1938).
15. Gayle Morrison, *To Move the World,* p. 37.
16. Ibid., pp. 275, 290.
17. Louis Lomax, *The Negro Revolt,* p. 19.
18. Louis Venters, *No Jim Crow Church: The Origins of South Carolina's Bahá'í Community,* p. 30.
19. Gayle Morrison, *To Move the World,* pp. 11, 14.
20. Shoghi Effendi, quoted in Gayle Morrison, *To Move the World,* p. 177.
21. Gayle Morrison, *To Move the World,* p. 13.
22. Ibid., p. 8.
23. Janet Ruhe-Schoen, *Champions of Oneness: Louis Gregory and His Shining Circle,* pp. 26, 29.
24. Gayle Morrison, *To Move the World,* p. 13.
25. Matthew 12:34.
26. Louis Gregory, quoted by a participant [name unknown] in Doris McKay, *Fires in Many Hearts,* p. 97.
27. Individual [name unknown], quoted in Doris McKay, *Fires in Many Hearts,* p. 97.
28. Louis Gregory, quoted by an individual [name unknown] in Doris McKay, *Fires in Many Hearts,* p. 97.
29. Louis Gregory, "Racial Amity in America: An Historical Review," in *Lights of the Spirit: Historical Portraits of Black Bahá'ís in North America, 1898–2000,* p. 178.
30. Louis Gregory, quoted in Janet Ruhe-Schoen, *Champions of Oneness: Louis Gregory and His Shining Circle,* p. 26.
31. Ibid., pp. 25–26.
32. Ibid., p. 25.

33. Gayle Morrison, *To Move the World,* p. 8.
34. Ibid., p. 12.
35. Louis Gregory, quoted in Gayle Morrison, *To Move the World,* p. 12.
36. Ibid., p. 11.
37. Gayle Morrison, *To Move the World,* p. 11.
38. Ibid.
39. Ibid., p. 87.
40. Louis Gregory, quoted in Gayle Morrison, *To Move the World,* p. 11.
41. Roy Williams, quoted in Janet Ruhe-Schoen, *Champions of Oneness: Louis Gregory and His Shining Circle,* p. 149.

2 / Education: A Lever for Social Change

1. Janet Ruhe-Schoen, *Champions of Oneness: Louis Gregory and His Shining Circle,* p. 30.
2. Janet Fleming Rose, *A Seed in Your Heart: The Life of Louise Mathew Gregory,* p. 3.
3. Louis Gregory, "Racial Amity in America An Historical Review," in Gwendolyn Etter-Lewis and Richard Thomas, *Lights of the Spirit: Historical Portraits of Black Bahá'ís in North America, 1898–2000,* p. 176.
4. "The Freedmen's Bureau," African American Heritage section of National Archives, https://www.archives.gov/research/african-americans/freedmens-bureau.
5. "Avery Institute History," https://www.averyinstitute.us/history.html.
6. Louis Venters, *No Jim Crow Church: The Origins of South Carolina's Bahá'í Community,* p. 33.
7. Janet Ruhe-Schoen, *Champions of Oneness: Louis Gregory and His Shining Circle,* pp. 28–29.
8. Ibid., p. 32.
9. Louis Gregory, quoted in Janet Ruhe-Schoen, *Champions of Oneness: Louis Gregory and His Shining Circle,* p. 32.
10. Gayle Morrison, *To Move the World,* pp. 15–16.

11. Louis Gregory, quoted in Gayle Morrison, *To Move the World,* p. 15.
12. Ibid.
13. "Denmark Vesey," National Park Service, https://www.nps.gov/people/denmark-vesey.htm.
14. Ibid.
15. Louis Venters, *No Jim Crow Church: The Origins of South Carolina's Bahá'í Community,* p. 32.
16. Louis Lomax, *The Negro Revolt,* p. 30.
17. Gayle Morrison, *To Move the World,* p. 14.
18. Louis Venters, *No Jim Crow Church: The Origins of South Carolina's Bahá'í Community,* p. 32.
19. Gayle Morrison, *To Move the World,* pp. 14–15.
20. Ibid., p. 14.
21. Louis Lomax, *The Negro Revolt,* pp. 14–15.
22. Louis Venters, *No Jim Crow Church: The Origins of South Carolina's Bahá'í Community,* p. 33.
23. See Jones-Radgowski's book titled *The Escape of Robert Smalls,* and https://freedomcenter.org/voice/robert-smalls/.
24. Ibid.
25. Gayle Morrison, *To Move the World,* p. 14.
26. 'Abdu'l-Bahá, quoted in Gayle Morrison, *To Move the World,* p. 52.
27. Shoghi Effendi, *The World Order of Bahá'u'lláh,* p. 43.
28. Gayle Morrison, *To Move the World,* pp. 3–4.
29. J. Clay Smith, Jr., *Emancipation: The Making of the Black Lawyer, 1844–1944,* p. 148.
30. Glenford Mitchell, in Gayle Morrison, *To Move the World,* pp. xv–xvi.

3 / Truth Had a Hearing

1. Gayle Morrison, *To Move the World,* pp. 4, 19, 27.
2. Ibid., p. 19.
3. Louis Gregory, quoted in Gayle Morrison, *To Move the World,* p. 16.

4. Glenford Mitchell, in Gayle Morrison, *To Move the World*, p. xv.
5. Louis Venters, *No Jim Crow Church: The Origins of South Carolina's Bahá'í Community*, p. 18.
6. Louis Gregory, quoted in Gayle Morrison, *To Move the World*, p. 19.
7. Ibid.
8. Louis Gregory, quoted in Janet Ruhe-Schoen, *Champions of Oneness: Louis Gregory and His Shining Circle*, p. 42.
9. Louis Gregory, quoted in Gayle Morrison, *To Move the World*, p. 24.
10. Ibid.
11. Ibid.
12. Gayle Morrison, *To Move the World*, p. 19.
13. Louis Gregory, quoted in Gayle Morrison, *To Move the World*, p. 26.
14. Ibid., p. 25.
15. Ibid., p. 26.
16. Louis Venters, *No Jim Crow Church: The Origins of South Carolina's Bahá'í Community*, pp. 18–19.
17. Louis Gregory, quoted in Louis Venters, *No Jim Crow Church: The Origins of South Carolina's Bahá'í Community*, p. 20.
18. Janet Ruhe-Schoen, *Champions of Oneness: Louis Gregory and His Shining Circle*, p. 61.
19. Ibid., p. 61.
20. Shoghi Effendi, *God Passes By*, p. 220.
21. Bahá'u'lláh, The Hidden Words, Arabic no. 68.
22. Janet Ruhe-Schoen, *Champions of Oneness: Louis Gregory and His Shining Circle*, p. 61; Paul Kingston Dealy, "The Dawn of Knowledge and Most Great Peace," https://bahai-library.com/dealy_dawn_knowledge/.
23. Louis Gregory, quoted in Gayle Morrison, *To Move the World*, p. 4.
24. Gayle Morrison, *To Move the World*, p. 26.
25. Louis Venters, *No Jim Crow Church: The Origins of South Carolina's Bahá'í Community*, p. 22.

26. Louis Gregory, quoted in Gayle Morrison, *To Move the World,* p. 5.
27. Ibid., p. 6.
28. Gayle Morrison, *To Move the World,* p. 27.
29. Ibid., p. 25; Louis Gregory, quoted in Gayle Morrison, *To Move the World,* p. 25.
30. Louis Gregory, quoted in Gayle Morrison, *To Move the World,* p. 110.
31. Ibid., p. 6.
32. Ibid., pp. 24, 19.
33. Bahá'u'lláh, The Hidden Words, Arabic no. 2.
34. Gayle Morrison, *To Move the World,* pp. 3–4.

4 / A Spiritual Foundation for Advancing Human Oneness

1. Gayle Morrison, *To Move the World,* pp. 8, 16.
2. George Gregory, quoted in Louis Venters, *No Jim Crow Church: The Origins of South Carolina's Bahá'í Community,* p. 118.
3. 'Abdu'l-Bahá, *Selections from the Writings of 'Abdu'l-Bahá,* no. 78.2.
4. Richard Thomas, in Gwendolyn Etter-Lewis and Richard Thomas, *Lights of the Spirit: Historical Portraits of Black Bahá'ís in North America, 1898–2000,* p. 38.
5. Ibid., p. 23.
6. Gayle Morrison, *To Move the World,* p. 29.
7. 'Abdu'l-Bahá, *The Promulgation of Universal Peace,* pp. 600–601.
8. Shoghi Effendi, quoted in Gwendolyn Etter-Lewis and Richard Thomas, *Lights of the Spirit: Historical Portraits of Black Bahá'ís in North America, 1898–2000,* p. 41.
9. Rúḥíyyih Khánum, quoted in Gwendolyn Etter-Lewis and Richard Thomas, *Lights of the Spirit: Historical Portraits of Black Bahá'ís in North America, 1898–2000,* p. 22.
10. Gayle Morrison, *To Move the World,* p. 195.

11. Race Amity Committee, "Annual Committee Reports," *Bahá'í News*, no. 88 (November, 1934): 10, https://bahai.works/Bah%C3%A1%E2%80%99%C3%AD_News/Issue_88/Text.
12. Ibid.
13. Joseph Hannen, quoted in Gayle Morrison, *To Move the World*, p. 32.
14. Gayle Morrison, *To Move the World*, p. 42.
15. Ibid., p. 27.
16. Louis Venters, *No Jim Crow Church: The Origins of South Carolina's Bahá'í Community*, p. 48.
17. 'Abdu'l-Bahá, *Paris Talks*, no. 15.12.
18. Louis G. Gregory Bahá'í Museum website, https://www.louisgregorymuseum.org/louis-g-gregory.
19. Gayle Morrison, *To Move the World*, p. 298.
20. Barron Harper, *Lights of Fortitude*, p. 85.
21. Louis Gregory, quoted in Gayle Morrison, *To Move the World*, p. 30.
22. Louis Gregory, quoted in Louis Venters, *No Jim Crow Church: The Origins of South Carolina's Bahá'í Community*, p. 36.
23. Roscoe Conkling Bruce, quoted in Louis Venters, *No Jim Crow Church: The Origins of South Carolina's Bahá'í Community*, p. 36.
24. Ibid.
25. Louis Gregory, quoted in Louis Venters, *No Jim Crow Church: The Origins of South Carolina's Bahá'í Community*, p. 37.
26. Gayle Morrison, *To Move the World*, p. 30.
27. Louis Gregory, quoted in Gayle Morrison, *To Move the World*, p. 30.
28. Gayle Morrison, *To Move the World*, p. 34.
29. Louis Gregory, quoted in Gayle Morrison, *To Move the World*, p. 5.
30. Ibid., p. 6.
31. Louis Venters, *No Jim Crow Church: The Origins of South Carolina's Bahá'í Community*, p. 28.

32. Richard Thomas, in Gwendolyn Etter-Lewis and Richard Thomas, *Lights of the Spirit: Historical Portraits of Black Bahá'ís in North America, 1898–2000,* p. 28.
33. Louis Gregory, quoted in Gayle Morrison, *To Move the World,* p. 6.
34. Ibid., p. 196.
35. Richard Newman, *Freedom's Prophet-Bishop Richard Allen, the AME Church, and the Black Founding Fathers,* pp. 21, 160.
36. Louis Venters, *No Jim Crow Church: The Origins of South Carolina's Bahá'í Community,* p. 29.
37. Joseph and Pauline Hannen, quoted in Gayle Morrison, *To Move the World,* p. 6.
38. Gayle Morrison, *To Move the World,* p. 6.
39. Louis Venters, *No Jim Crow Church: The Origins of South Carolina's Bahá'í Community,* p. 28.
40. Ibid., p. 48.
41. Ibid.
42. Ibid.
43. "Evolution of the U.S. Community: The Growth of the Bahá'í Faith in America," https://www.bahai.us/beliefs/origins/evolution/#:~:text=The%20National%20Spiritual%20Assembly%20of,the%20United%20States%20in%201922.
44. Barron Harper, *Lights of Fortitude,* p. 94.

5 / Pilgrimage

1. Louis Venters, *No Jim Crow Church: The Origins of South Carolina's Bahá'í Community,* p. 48.
2. Gayle Morrison, *To Move the World,* pp. 42–43.
3. Ibid., p. 41.
4. 'Abdu'l-Bahá, quoted in Gayle Morrison, *To Move the World,* p. 47.
5. Gayle Morrison, *To Move the World,* p. 42.
6. Louis Gregory, quoted in Janet Ruhe-Schoen, *Champions of Oneness: Louis Gregory and His Shining Circle,* p. 83.
7. Gayle Morrison, *To Move the World,* pp. 42–43.

8. Louis Gregory, quoted in Gayle Morrison, *To Move the World,* p. 43.
9. Gayle Morrison, *To Move the World,* p. 43.
10. Ibid., p. 42.
11. Louis Gregory, quoted in Janet Ruhe-Schoen, *Champions of Oneness: Louis Gregory and His Shining Circle,* p. 84.
12. Ibid.
13. Louis Venters, *No Jim Crow Church: The Origins of South Carolina's Bahá'í Community,* p. 49.
14. Ibid.
15. Christopher Columbus, quoted in Jill Lepore, *These Truths: A History of the United States,* pp. 3, 4, 5, 12, 13.
16. Ibid., p. 13.
17. Ibid., pp. 3, 4, 5, 12, 13.
18. Ibid., p. 13.
19. 'Abdu'l-Bahá, *Foundations of World Unity,* p. 108.
20. Houston Smith, *The World's Religions,* p. 365.
21. 'Abdu'l-Bahá, *Foundations of World Unity,* p. 108.
22. Moojan Momen, quoted in Janet Ruhe-Schoen, *Champions of Oneness: Louis Gregory and His Shining Circle,* p. 59.
23. Janet Ruhe-Schoen, *Champions of Oneness: Louis Gregory and His Shining Circle,* p. 83.
24. Louis Gregory, quoted in Gayle Morrison, *To Move the World,* p. 44.
25. 'Abdu'l-Bahá, quoted in Louis Gregory, *A Heavenly Vista,* p. 10, https://bahai-library.com/pdf/g/gregory_heavenly_vista.pdf.
26. Louis Gregory, quoted in Louis Gregory, *A Heavenly Vista,* p. 10, https://bahai-library.com/pdf/g/gregory_heavenly_vista.pdf.
27. Louis Gregory, *A Heavenly Vista,* p. 10, https://bahai-library.com/pdf/g/gregory_heavenly_vista.pdf.
28. Gayle Morrison, *To Move the World,* p. 64.
29. 'Abdu'l-Bahá, quoted in Gayle Morrison, *To Move the World,* p. 45.

30. Ibid., p. 46.
31. 'Abdu'l-Bahá, quoted in Janet Ruhe-Schoen, *Champions of Oneness: Louis Gregory and His Shining Circle,* p. 93.
32. Ibid.
33. Louis Gregory, quoted in Janet Ruhe-Schoen, *Champions of Oneness: Louis Gregory and His Shining Circle,* p. 93.
34. 'Abdu'l-Bahá, quoted in Janet Ruhe-Schoen, *Champions of Oneness: Louis Gregory and His Shining Circle,* p. 93.
35. 'Abdu'l-Bahá, quoted by translator [name unknown] in Janet Ruhe-Schoen, *Champions of Oneness: Louis Gregory and His Shining Circle,* p. 93.
36. Ibid., p. 86.
37. Louis Gregory, quoted in Janet Ruhe-Schoen, *Champions of Oneness: Louis Gregory and His Shining Circle,* p. 86.
38. Gayle Morrison, *To Move the World,* p. 46.
39. 'Abdu'l-Bahá, quoted in Gayle Morrison, *To Move the World,* p. 47.
40. Ibid., pp. 47–48.
41. Ibid., p. 48.

6 / A Special Marriage Encouraged by 'Abdu'l-Bahá

1. Janet Ruhe-Schoen, *Champions of Oneness: Louis Gregory and His Shining Circle,* p. 99.
2. Gayle Morrison, *To Move the World,* p. 50.
3. 'Abdu'l-Bahá, quoted in Gayle Morrison, *To Move the World,* p. 50.
4. Gayle Morrison, *To Move the World,* p. 50.
5. Janet Ruhe-Schoen, *Champions of Oneness: Louis Gregory and His Shining Circle,* p. 100.
6. Gayle Morrison, *To Move the World,* p. 50.
7. Janet Fleming Rose, *A Seed in Your Heart: The Life of Louise Mathew Gregory,* p. 19.
8. Janet Ruhe-Schoen, *Champions of Oneness: Louis Gregory and His Shining Circle,* p. 84.
9. Gayle Morrison, *To Move the World,* p. 43.

10. Louise Gregory, quoted in Janet Fleming Rose, *A Seed in Your Heart: The Life of Louise Mathew Gregory,* p. 25.
11. Janet Fleming Rose, *A Seed in Your Heart: The Life of Louise Mathew Gregory,* p. 25.
12. Ibid., p. 31.
13. Janet Fleming Rose; *A Seed in Your Heart: The Life of Louise Mathew Gregory,* p. 30; Janet Ruhe-Schoen, *Champions of Oneness: Louis Gregory and His Shining Circle,* p. 125.
14. Janet Ruhe-Schoen, *Champions of Oneness: Louis Gregory and His Shining Circle,* p. 125.
15. 'Abdu'l-Bahá, quoted in Janet Fleming Rose, *A Seed in Your Heart: The Life of Louise Mathew Gregory,* pp. 31–34.
16. Ibid., p. 49.
17. See Janet Fleming Rose, *A Seed in Your Heart: The Life of Louise Mathew Gregory,* pp. 24–35, for additional virtues and strengths that "marked her out as especially suitable for such a difficult enterprise as an interracial marriage in the early 20th century" (p. 76).
18. Gayle Morrison, *To Move the World,* p. 63.
19. Ibid.
20. Louise Mathew, quoted in Gayle Morrison, *To Move the World,* pp. 66–67.
21. Reported words of 'Abdu'l-Bahá, Louise, and Louis quoted by Louise in Gayle Morrison, *To Move the World,* p. 67.
22. Janet Ruhe-Schoen, *Champions of Oneness: Louis Gregory and His Shining Circle,* pp. 130–31.
23. Ibid., p. 131.
24. Ibid.
25. 'Abdu'l-Bahá, in *Bahá'í Prayers,* p. 120; see also "The first Inter-racial Baha'i Marriage," https://www-dev.bahai.us/21936/.
26. Gayle Morrison, *To Move the World,* p. 72.
27. 'Abdu'l-Bahá, quoted in Gayle Morrison, *To Move the World,* p. 72.
28. Shoghi Effendi, *God Passes By,* p. 457.

29. Gayle Morrison, *To Move the World,* p. 62.
30. Janet Ruhe-Schoen, *Champions of Oneness: Louis Gregory and His Shining Circle,* p. 134.
31. Ibid., p. 158.
32. Janet Fleming Rose, *A Seed in Your Heart: The Life of Louise Mathew Gregory,* p. 107.
33. Gayle Morrison, *To Move the World,* p. 71.
34. Louis Gregory, quoted in Gayle Morrison, *To Move the World,* p. 89.
35. Ibid., p. 71.
36. Gayle Morrison, *To Move the World,* p. 90.
37. Ibid.
38. Louise Gregory, quoted in Gayle Morrison, *To Move the World,* p. 90.
39. Ibid., p. 86.
40. Gayle Morrison, *To Move the World,* p. 64.
41. Janet Fleming Rose, *A Seed in Your Heart: The Life of Louise Mathew Gregory,* p. 86.
42. Louis Gregory quoted in Gayle Morrison, *To Move the World,* p. 70.
43. Ibid.
44. Gayle Morrison, *To Move the World,* p. 70.
45. Janet Fleming Rose, *A Seed in Your Heart: The Life of Louise Mathew Gregory,* p. 93.
46. Janet Ruhe-Schoen, *Champions of Oneness: Louis Gregory and His Shining Circle,* p. 143.
47. Gwendolyn Etter-Lewis, in Gwendolyn Etter-Lewis and Richard Thomas, *Lights of the Spirit: Historical Portraits of Black Bahá'ís in North America, 1898–2000,* p. 71; Gayle Morrison, *To Move the World,* p. 166.
48. Ibid.
49. Ibid.
50. Coralie Franklin Cook, letter to 'Abdu'l-Bahá 'Abbás, quoted in Gwendolyn Etter Lewis and Richard Thomas, *Lights of the*

Spirit: Historical Portraits of Black Bahá'ís in North America, 1898–2000, pp. 237–38.

51. Ibid., pp. 239–40.
52. Louise Mathews, quoted in Janet Fleming Rose, *A Seed in Your Heart: The Life of Louise Mathew Gregory,* p. 78.
53. Janet Fleming Rose, *A Seed in Your Heart: The Life of Louise Mathew Gregory,* pp. 71–72.
54. 'Abdu'l-Bahá, quoted in Janet Fleming Rose, *A Seed in Your Heart: The Life of Louise Mathew Gregory,* p. 88.
55. Janet Fleming Rose, *A Seed in Your Heart: The Life of Louise Mathew Gregory,* p. 14.

7 / Compelling Lessons from 'Abdu'l-Bahá about Oneness

1. Gayle Morrison, *To Move the World,* p. 87.
2. Ibid., p. 52.
3. Louis Gregory, quoted in Gayle Morrison, *To Move the World,* p. 52.
4. Gayle Morrison, *To Move the World,* p. 53.
5. Harlan Ober, quoted in Gayle Morrison, *To Move the World,* p. 53.
6. Gayle Morrison, *To Move the World,* p. 53.
7. Harlan Ober, quoted in Gayle Morrison, *To Move the World,* p. 53.
8. Louis Gregory, quoted in Gayle Morrison, *To Move the World,* p. 53.
9. Ibid., p. 53.
10. Janet Ruhe-Schoen, *Champions of Oneness: Louis Gregory and His Shining Circle,* p. 102.
11. Howard University Law School, https://law.howard.edu.
12. Louis Gregory, quoted in Gwendolyn Etter-Lewis and Richard Thomas, *Lights of the Spirit: Historical Portraits of Black Bahá'ís in North America, 1898–2000,* p. 179.
13. Ibid., pp. 179–80.
14. 'Abdu'l-Bahá, *The Promulgation of Universal Peace,* pp. 60–63.

15. Gayle Morrison, *To Move the World,* pp. 55–56.
16. 'Abdu'l-Bahá, quoted in Mírzá Maḥmúd-i-Zarqáni, *Maḥmud's Diary: The Diary of Mírzá Maḥmúd-i-Zarqání Chronicling 'Abdu'l-Bahá's Journey to America,* p. 364.
17. Gayle Morrison, *To Move the World,* p. 57.
18. Louis Gregory, quoted in Gayle Morrison, *To Move the World,* p. 57.
19. Gayle Morrison, *To Move the World,* pp. 57–58.
20. 'Abdu'l-Bahá, Louis Gregory, and Gayle Morrison, quoted in Gayle Morrison, *To Move the World,* p. 60.
21. Ibid., pp. 60–61.
22. Louis Gregory, quoted in Gayle Morrison, *To Move the World,* p. 57.
23. Gayle Morrison, *To Move the World,* p. 86.
24. Roy Williams, quoted in Janet Ruhe-Schoen, *Champions of Oneness: Louis Gregory and His Shining Circle,* p. 162.
25. Gayle Morrison, *To Move the World,* p. 86.
26. Louis Gregory, quoted in Gayle Morrison, *To Move the World,* pp. 86–87.
27. Gayle Morrison, *To Move the World,* p. 87.
28. Ibid., p. 88.
29. Ibid., p. 87.
30. Shoghi Effendi, quoted in Gwendolyn Etter-Lewis and Richard Thomas, *Lights of the Spirit: Historical Portraits of Black Bahá'ís in North America, 1898–2000,* p. 280.
31. Shoghi Effendi, *The World Order of Bahá'u'lláh,* p. 134.
32. Shoghi Effendi, *The Advent of Divine Justice,* ¶52.
33. Unnamed individual, quoted in 'Abdu'l-Bahá, *'Abdu'l-Bahá in London,* p. 68.
34. 'Abdu'l-Bahá, quoted in *'Abdu'l-Bahá in London,* p. 68.
35. 'Abdu'l-Bahá, *The Promulgation of Universal Peace,* pp. 265–66.

8 / Serving Human Oneness Under the Divine Plan

1. Gayle Morrison, *To Move the World,* p. 296.

2. Letter written on behalf of Shoghi Effendi, quoted in Gayle Morrison, *To Move the World*, p. 296.
3. Ibid.
4. Gayle Morrison, *To Move the World*, p. 296.
5. Ibid., p. 4.
6. Harlan Ober, "LOUIS G. GREGORY," *The Bahá'í World*, vol. 12, (1950–1954): 666–70.
7. Barron Harper, *Lights of Fortitude*, p. 97.
8. Shoghi Effendi, *The World Order of Bahá'u'lláh*, p. 194.
9. Harland Ober, quoted in Barron Harper, *Lights of Fortitude*, p. 93.
10. Gayle Morrison, *To Move the World*, pp. 318–19.
11. Louis Gregory, quoted in Gayle Morrison, *To Move the World*, p. 61.
12. Ibid., pp. 262–63.
13. Shoghi Effendi, *The Advent of Divine Justice*.
14. Louis Gregory, quoted in Gayle Morrison, *To Move the World*, p. 263.
15. Ibid.
16. Gayle Morrison, *To Move the World*, p. 84.
17. Ibid., p. 319.
18. Shoghi Effendi, *The Advent of Divine Justice*, ¶38.
19. Ibid., ¶51.
20. Gayle Morrison, *To Move the World*, p. 190.
21. Doris McKay, *Fires in Many Hearts*, p. 175.
22. Gwendolyn Etter-Lewis and Richard Thomas, *Lights of the Spirit: Historical Portraits of Black Bahá'ís in North America, 1898–2000*, p. 199.
23. Willard McKay, quoted in ibid., p. 182.
24. Doris McKay and Willard McKay, quoted in Doris McKay, *Fires in Many Hearts*, p. 182.
25. Janet Ruhe-Schoen, "An Early Freedom Ride, 1931: Louis Gregory and William McKay," p. 8, https://www.academia.edu/16404969/An_Early_Freedom_Ride_1931_Louis_Gregory_and_Willard_McKay.

26. Letter written on behalf of Shoghi Effendi, in Helen Hornby, *Lights of Guidance,* p. 529.
27. 'Abdu'l-Bahá, *The Promulgation of Universal Peace,* p. 611.
28. Willard McKay, quoted in Doris McKay, *Fires in Many Hearts,* pp. 182, 184.
29. George Washington Carver, quoted in Richard Thomas, Gwendolyn Etter-Lewis and Richard Thomas, *Lights of the Spirit: Historical Portraits of Black Bahá'ís in North America, 1898–2000,* p. 32.
30. Louis Gregory, quoted in Janet Ruhe-Schoen, *Champions of Oneness: Louis Gregory and His Shining Circle,* p. 240.
31. Willard McKay, quoted in Janet Ruhe-Schoen, *Champions of Oneness: Louis Gregory and His Shining Circle,* p. 241.
32. Shoghi Effendi, quoted in Janet Ruhe-Schoen, *Champions of Oneness: Louis Gregory and His Shining Circle,* p. 241.
33. Charles Wagg, quoted in Gayle Morrison, *To Move the World,* p. 318.
34. Letter dated January 28, 1933 written on behalf of Shoghi Effendi to Mr. Charles Wragg (previously unpublished).
35. 'Abdu'l-Bahá, *Tablets of the Divine Plan,* pp. 9–12, 67–73.
36. Gayle Morrison, *To Move the World,* p. 100.
37. Louis Venters, *No Jim Crow Church: The Origins of South Carolina's Bahá'í Community,* p. 78.
38. Roy Williams, quoted in Janet Ruhe-Schoen, *Champions of Oneness: Louis Gregory and His Shining Circle,* p. 153.
39. Janet Ruhe-Schoen, *Champions of Oneness: Louis Gregory and His Shining Circle,* p. 161.
40. Ibid., pp. 159–60; Gayle Morrison, *To Move the World,* p. 103.
41. Janet Ruhe-Shoen, *Champions of Oneness: Louis Gregory and His Shining Circle,* p. 160.
42. Ibid., p. 156.
43. Gayle Morrison, *To Move the World,* p. 115.
44. Ibid., p. 122.
45. 'Abdu'l-Bahá, *The Promulgation of Universal Peace,* pp. 96–97.

46. Gayle Morrison, *To Move the World,* p. 118.
47. Louis Gregory, quoted in Gayle Morrison, *To Move the World,* p. 118.
48. Ibid., pp. 118–19.
49. Gayle Morrison, *To Move the World,* pp. 119–20.
50. The Local Spiritual Assembly of Seattle, quoted in Gayle Morrison, *To Move the World,* p. 120.
51. Gayle Morrison, *To Move the World,* pp. 120–21.
52. Ibid., p. 121.
53. The National Teaching Committee, quoted in Gayle Morrison, *To Move the World,* p. 122.
54. Gayle Morrison, *To Move the World,* p. 117.
55. Mariam Haney, quoted in Gayle Morrison, *To Move the World,* p. 117.
56. Ibid., p. 117.
57. Gayle Morrison, *To Move the World,* p. 116.
58. Ibid.
59. Gayle Morrison, "A New Creation: The Power of the Covenant in the Life of Louis Gregory." *Journal of Bahá'í Studies,* Vol. 9, Number 4, 1994, p. 1, https://journal.bahaistudies.ca/online/article/view/8/6.
60. Ibid., p. 2.
61. Horace Holley, quoted in Gayle Morrison, *To Move the World,* p. 316. For a full report of Mr. Gregory's achievements during this extensive teaching tour, see Gayle Morrison, *To Move the World,* pp. 114–22.
62. Gayle Morrison, *To Move the World,* p. xxiii.
63. Elsie Austin, *Above All Barriers,* pp. 1–2.
64. Louis Gregory, "Racial Amity in America: An Historical Review." In Gwendolyn Etter-Lewis and Richard Thomas, *Lights of the Spirit: Historical Portraits of Black Bahá'ís in North America, 1898–2000,* pp. 180–201 and *The Bahá'í World* (1936–38) and Janet Ruhe-Shoen, *Champions of Oneness: Louis Gregory and His Shining Circle,* pp. 198–200.

65. Janet Ruhe-Shoen, *Champions of Oneness: Louis Gregory and His Shining Circle,* p. 197.
66. Louis Gregory, quoted in Gayle Morrison, *To Move the World,* p. 121.
67. Ibid. p. 131.
68. Ibid., p. 135.
69. Words of 'Abdu'l-Bahá, reported by Mountfort Mills and quoted in Gayle Morrison, *To Move the World,* p. 141.
70. Louis Gregory, quoted in Gayle Morrison, *To Move the World,* p. 132.
71. Minutes of the Executive Board of Bahá'í Temple Unity dated 11 Sept. 1919, quoted in Gayle Morrison, *To Move the World,* p. 131.
72. Ibid, pp. 196–97.
73. Words of Senator Moses Clapp recorded in the Proceedings of the Annual Meeting of the Bahai Temple Unity, 1922, p. 308, quoted in Gayle Morrison, *To Move the World,* p. 137.
74. Louis Gregory, quoted in Gayle Morrison, *To Move the World,* p. 138.
75. Gayle Morrison, *To Move the World,* p. 141.
76. Ibid., pp. 140–41.
77. Ibid., pp. 139, 141.
78. Janet Ruhe-Shoen, *Champions of Oneness: Louis Gregory and His Shining Circle,* p. 193.
79. Louis Gregory, quoted in Gayle Morrison, *To Move the World,* p. 138.
80. Ibid., p. 134.
81. Louis Gregory, quoted in Janet Ruhe-Schoen, *Champions of Oneness: Louis Gregory and His Shining Circle,* p. 193.
82. Louis Gregory, *Racial Amity in America: An Historical Review,* pp. 175–201.
83. Gayle Morrison, *To Move the World,* p. 142.
84. Ibid.
85. 'Abdu'l-Bahá, quoted in Gayle Morrison, *To Move the World,* p. 142.

86. Ibid., p. 143.
87. W. E. B. DuBois, quoted in Gayle Morrison, *To Move the World,* p. 193.
88. Walter White, quoted in Gayle Morrison, *To Move the World,* p. 192.
89. Bessye Bearden, "New York Society," Chicago Defender, 5 Mar. 1932, p. 1, quoted in Gayle Morrison, *To Move the World,* pp. 192–93.
90. Gayle Morrison, *To Move the World,* pp. 192–93.
91. "The Epochs of the Formative Age," enclosed with a letter dated 5 February 1986 from the Universal House of Justice to all National Spiritual Assemblies.
92. Gayle Morrison, *To Move the World,* pp. 247–250; Janet Ruhe-Schoen, *Champions of Oneness: Louis Gregory and His Shining Circle,* pp. 206–7.
93. Louis Venters, *No Jim Crow Church: The Origins of South Carolina's Bahá'í Community,* pp. 190–91.
94. Judge Waties Waring, quoted in Louis Venters, *No Jim Crow Church: The Origins of South Carolina's Bahá'í Community,* pp. 190–91.
95. Louis Venters, *No Jim Crow Church: The Origins of South Carolina's Bahá'í Community,* p. 191.

9 / A Man for Serving Oneness

1. Bahá'u'lláh, *Gleanings from the Writings of Bahá'u'lláh,* no. 117.1.
2. 'Abdu'l-Bahá, *Paris Talks,* no. 45.13.
3. 'Abdu'l-Bahá, quoted in Gayle Morrison, *To Move the World,* p. 55.
4. 'Abdu'l-Bahá, *The Secret of Divine Civilization,* ¶182.
5. Gayle Morrison, *To Move the World,* p. 318.
6. 'Abdu'l-Bahá, *The Promulgation of Universal Peace,* pp. 638–39.
7. Janet Ruhe-Schoen, *Champions of Oneness: Louis Gregory and His Shining Circle,* p. 192.

8. Louis Gregory, quoted in Janet Ruhe-Schoen, *Champions of Oneness: Louis Gregory and His Shining Circle,* p. 192.
9. Pauline Hannen, quoted in Gayle Morrison, *To Move the World,* pp. 26–27.
10. Gayle Morrison, *To Move the World,* p. xxiii.
11. Bahá'u'lláh, *Gleanings from the Writings of Bahá'u'lláh,* no. 16.1.
12. 'Abdu'l-Bahá, *The Promulgation of Universal Peace,* p. 474.
13. Louis Gregory, quoted in Gayle Morrison, *To Move the World,* p. 321.
14. 'Abdu'l-Bahá, *The Promulgation of Universal Peace,* pp. 167–68.
15. Shoghi Effendi, *Bahá'í Administration,* p. 129.
16. 'Abdu'l-Bahá, *Selections from the Writings of 'Abdu'l-Bahá,* no. 76.1.
17. 'Abdu'l-Bahá, quoted in Gayle Morrison, *To Move the World,* pp. 313–14.
18. Ibid., p. 314.
19. 'Abdu'l-Bahá, quoted in "In Memoriam to Louis G. Gregory," *The Bahá'í World,* (vol. 12): 667–68, https://bahai.works/Bah%C3%A1%E2%80%99%C3%AD_World/Volume_12/In_Memoriam.
20. Shoghi Effendi, quoted in Gayle Morrison, *To Move the World,* p. 317.
21. Ibid., p. 237.
22. Shoghi Effendi, letter written to Louis Gregory dated 4/4/25, in Bonnie Taylor, *The Pupil of the Eye: African Americans and the World Order of Bahá'u'lláh,* pp. 10–11.
23. Shoghi Effendi, quoted in Gayle Morrison, *To Move the World,* p. 177.
24. Universal House of Justice, from a letter to a believer dated September 2, 1992, quoted in Bonnie J. Taylor, *African Americans in the World Order of Bahá'u'lláh,* pp. 109–10.
25. Letter dated April 1, 1996 written on behalf of the Universal House of Justice to a believer, https://bahai-library.com/uhj_african_americans_us.

10 / Passing

1. Shoghi Effendi, *Citadel of Faith,* p. 163.
2. Gayle Morrison, *To Move the World,* p. 312.
3. Shoghi Effendi, *Citadel of Faith,* p. 164.
4. Gayle Morrison, *To Move the World,* p. 311.

BIBLIOGRAPHY

Works of Bahá'u'lláh

Epistle to the Son of the Wolf. Wilmette, IL: Bahá'í Publishing Trust, 1988.

Gleanings from the Writings of Bahá'u'lláh. New ed. Wilmette, IL: Bahá'í Publishing, 2005.

The Hidden Words. Wilmette, IL: Bahá'í Publishing, 2002.

Tablets of Bahá'u'lláh Revealed after the Kitáb-i-Aqdas. Compiled by the Research Department of the Universal House of Justice and translated by Habib Taherzadeh with the assistance of a Committee at the Bahá'í World Center. Wilmette, IL: Bahá'í Publishing Trust, 1988.

Works of 'Abdu'l-Bahá

'Abdu'l-Bahá in London. London: Bahá'í Publishing Trust, 1982.

Foundations of World Unity. Wilmette, IL: Bahá'í Publishing Trust, 1979.

Paris Talks: Addresses Given by 'Abdu'l-Bahá in Paris in 1911. 2024 reprint. Wilmette, IL: Bahá'í Publishing, 2006.

The Promulgation of Universal Peace. Wilmette, IL: Bahá'í Publishing Trust, 2007.

The Secret of Divine Civilization. Translated from the Persian by Marzieh Gail in consultation with Ali-Kuli Khan. Wilmette, IL: Bahá'í Publishing, 2015.

Selections from the Writings of 'Abdu'l-Bahá. Wilmette, IL: Bahá'í Publishing, 2010.

Tablets of the Divine Plan. Wilmette, IL: Bahá'í Publishing Trust, 1993.

The Will and Testament of 'Abdu'l-Bahá. 2002 reprint. Wilmette, IL: Bahá'í Publishing Trust, 1944.

Works of Shoghi Effendi

The Advent of Divine Justice. New ed. Wilmette, IL: Bahá'í Publishing Trust, 2006.

Citadel of Faith. Wilmette, IL: Bahá'í Publishing Trust, 2014.

God Passes By. Wilmette, IL: Bahá'í Publishing Trust, 2010.

The World Order of Bahá'u'lláh. Wilmette, IL: Bahá'í Publishing Trust, 1991.

Works of the Universal House of Justice

Letter dated April 1, 1996 written on behalf of the Universal House of Justice to a believer. https://bahai-library.com/uhj_african_americans_us.

Compilations

Bahá'u'lláh, the Báb, and 'Abdu'l-Bahá. *Bahá'í Prayers: A Selection of Prayers Revealed by Bahá'u'lláh, the Báb, and 'Abdu'l-Bahá.* Reprinted 2022. Wilmette, IL: Bahá'í Publishing Trust, 2002.

Other Works

Austin, Elsie. *Above All Barriers: The Story of Louis G. Gregory.* Wilmette: Bahá'í Publishing Trust, 1976. https://bahai-library.com/pdf/a/austin_above_all_barriers.pdf.

"Avery Institute History." https://www.averyinstitute.us/history.html.

Dealy, Paul Kingson. *The Dawn of Knowledge and Most Great Peace.* Chicago: Bahá'í Publishing Society, 1903. https://bahai-library.com/dealy_dawn_knowledge.

DuBois, W. E. B. *Black Reconstruction, an Essay Toward a History of the Part Which Black Folk Played in the Attempt to Reconstruct Democracy in America, 1860–1880.* First edition. Oxford: Oxford University Press, 2014.

Etter-Lewis, Gwendolyn and Richard Thomas, eds. *Lights of the Spirit: Historical Portraits of Black Bahá'ís in North America, 1898–2000.* Wilmette, IL: Bahá'í Publishing Trust, 2006.

"Evolution of the U.S. Community: The Growth of the Bahá'í Faith in America." https://www.bahai.us/beliefs/origins/evolution/#:~:text=The%20National%20Spiritual%20Assembly%20of,the%20United%20States%20in%201922.

"The first Inter-racial Baha'i Marriage." https://www-dev.bahai.us/21936/.

"The Freedmen's Bureau." African American Heritage section of National Archives. https://www.archives.gov/research/african-americans/freedmens-bureau.

Gregory, Louis. "A Gift of Race Enlightenment." *World Order.* Vol. 2 (1936).

———. "A Heavenly Vista: The Pilgrimage of Louis G. Gregory." Washington: R. L. Pendleton, 1911. https://bahai-library.com/gregory_heavenly_vista.

———. "Light on Basic Unity." *Bahá'í World.* Vol. 4 (1930–1932). https://bahai.works/Bah%C3%A1%E2%80%99%C3%AD_World/Volume_4/Light_on_Basic_Unity.

———. "Racial Amity in America: An Historical Review." *Bahá'í World.* Vol. 7 (1936–1938). https://bahai.works/Bahá'í_World/Volume_7/Racial_Amity_in_America.

Harper, Barron. *Lights of Fortitude.* Oxford: George Ronald, 2021.

Hornsby, Helen, ed. *Lights of Guidance: A Bahá'í Reference File.* Sixth Edition. New Delhi: Bahá'í Publishing Trust, 1999.

"Howard University School of Law." https://law.howard.edu.

"I'm So Glad Trouble Don't Last Always." Lyrics. https://www.negrospirituals.com/songs/i_m_so_glad_trouble_don_t_last_always.htm.

Jones-Radgowski, Jehan. *The Escape of Robert Small.* North Mankato, MN: Capstone Editions, 2019.

King James Bible. Nasvhille, Thomas Nelson Publishers: 1984.

Lepore, Jill. *These Truths: A History of the United States.* New York: W. W. Norton & Company, 2018.

Lomax, Louis E. *The Negro Revolt.* New York: Harper and Row, 1962.

McKay, Doris. *Fires in Many Hearts.* Oxford: George Ronald, 2021.

Mírzá Maḥmúd-i-Zarqání. *Maḥmúd's Diary: The Diary of Mírzá Maḥmúd-i-Zarqání Chronicling 'Abdu'l-Bahá's Journey to America.* Oxford: George Ronald, 1998.

Morrison, Gayle. *To Move the World: Louis G. Gregory and the Advancement of Racial Unity in America.* Wilmette, IL: Bahá'í Publishing Trust, 1995.

———. "A New Creation: The Power of the Covenant in the Life of Louis Gregory." *Journal of Bahá'í Studies.* Vol. 9, no. 4 (1995).

National Park Service. "Denmark Vesey." https://www.nps.gov/people/denmark-vesey.htm.

Newman, Richard S. *Freedom's Prophet-Bishop Richard Allen, the AME Church, and the Black Founding Fathers.* New York: New York University Press, 2008.

Ober, Harlan. "In Memoriam to Louis G. Gregory." *The Bahá'í World.* Volume XII (1950–1954). https://bahai.works/Bahá'í_World/Volume_12/In_Memoriam.

Rabbani, Rúḥíyyih. *The Guardian of the Bahá'í Faith.* Haifa, Israel: Bahá'í Publishing Trust, 1988.

Race Amity Committee. "Annual Committee Reports." *Bahá'í News,* no. 88 (November, 1934): 10. https://bahai.works/Bah%C3%A1%E2%80%99%C3%AD_News/Issue_88/Text.

Rose, Janet Fleming. *A Seed in Your Heart: The Life of Louise Mathew Gregory.* Oxford: George Ronald, 2018.

Ruhe-Schoen, Janet. *Champions of Oneness: Louis Gregory and His Shining Circle.* Wilmette, IL: Bahá'í Publishing Trust, 2015.

———. "An Early Freedom Ride, 1931: Louis Gregory and Willard McKay." https://www.academia.edu/16404969/An_Early_Freedom_Ride_1931_Louis_Gregory_and_Willard_McKay.

Smith, Huston. *The World's Religions.* New York: Harper One, 2009.

Smith Jr., J. Clay. *Emancipation: The Making of the Black Lawyer, 1844–1944.* Philadelphia: University of Pennsylvania Press, 1993.

Taylor, Bonnie J., comp. *The Pupil of the Eye: African Americans in the World Order of Bahá'u'lláh.* Rivera Beach: Palabra Publications, 1995.

Thomas, Richard W. "Changes in the Racial Status Quo: Challenges, Compromises, Resistance and Denial." *Racial Unity: An Imperative for Social Progress.* Ottawa: Association for Bahá'í Studies, 1993.

Venters, Louis. *No Jim Crow Church: The Origins of South Carolina's Bahá'í Community.* Gainesville, FL: University Press of Florida, 2015.

INDEX

B

C

P

R

S

V

W

ABOUT THE AUTHORS

Kiser Barnes holds a Juris Doctor Law Degree from the University of Maryland and a Master of Philosophy in Law from Awolowo University, Ife, Nigeria. His numerous publications include *Blessings of Service, Oneness,* "The Theme of Service in the Evolving World Order of Bahá'u'lláh," and "The Nature of Bahá'í Law." He remains inspired by Gayle Morrison's hope, written in his copy of her excellent book, *To Move the World: Louis G. Gregory and the Advancement of Racial Unity in America:* "May the light of unity that illuminated from Gregory's path guide you always.—Gayle Morrison, Haifa, 12 October 1995." He lives in Raleigh, North Carolina.

Linda Ahdieh Grant lives with her family in Decatur, Georgia. She holds a BA in Anthropology from Haverford College, a MPH in International Health from Emory School of Public Health, and a PhD in Epidemiology from Johns Hopkins School of Public Health. She has worked with others to create several children's books, including *I Love My Name, Sometimes I Made Him Laugh,* and *Zia's Search,* that aim to connect hearts with heroes and heroines from Bahá'í history, and she has co-founded a publishing company, One Heart Books.